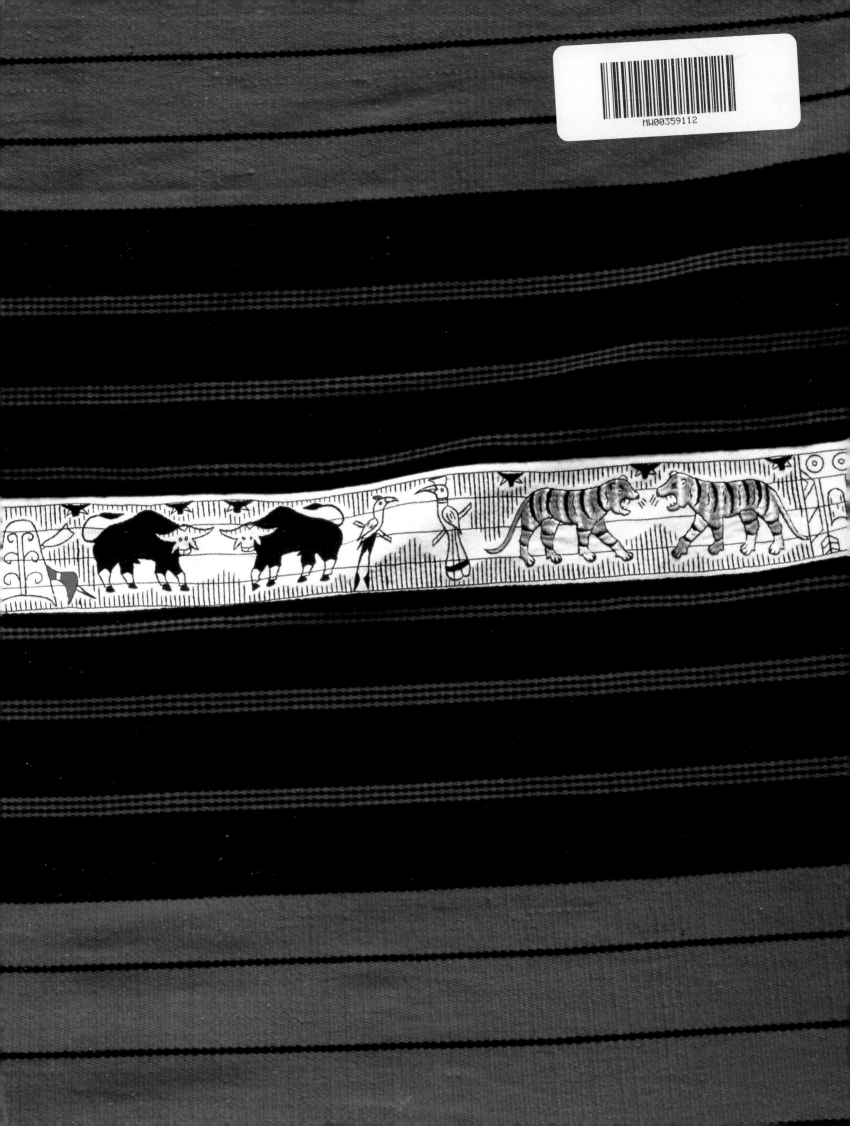

THE SEVEN SISTERS OF
INDIA

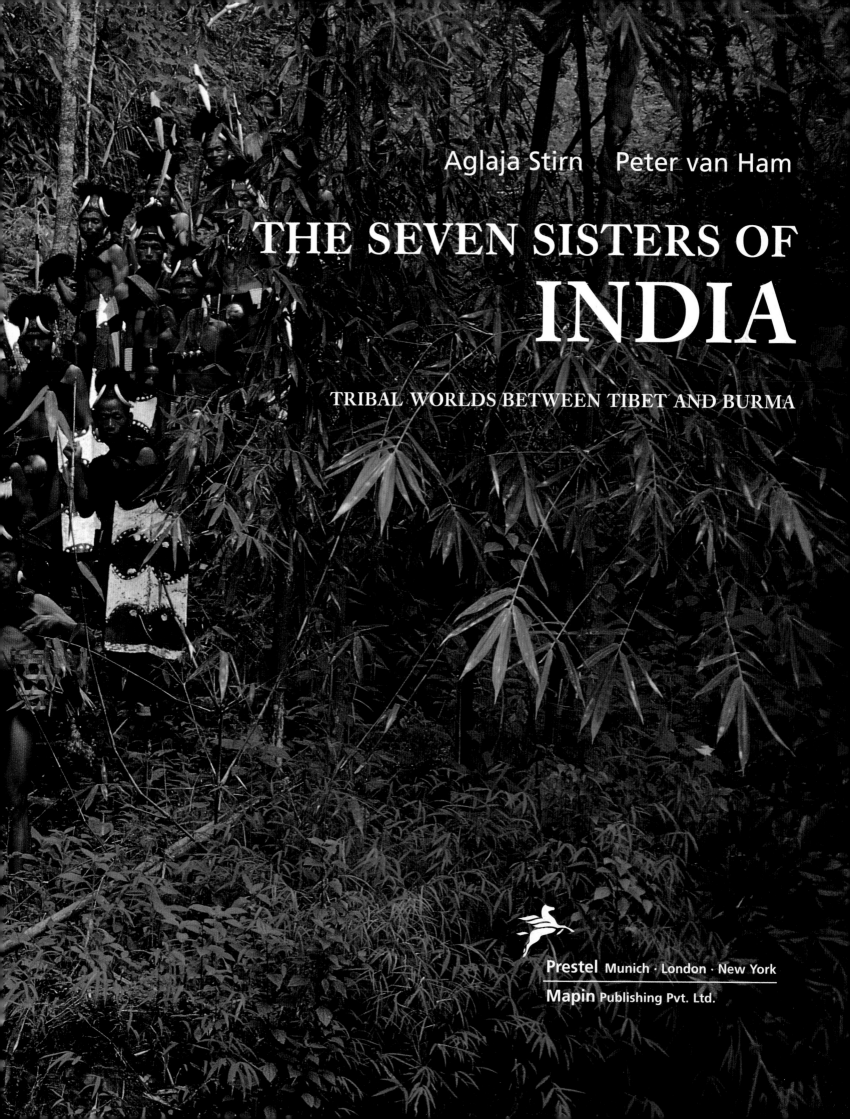

Aglaja Stirn   Peter van Ham

THE SEVEN SISTERS OF
INDIA

TRIBAL WORLDS BETWEEN TIBET AND BURMA

Prestel Munich · London · New York

Mapin Publishing Pvt. Ltd.

Back cover: Suspension bridge in northern Arunachal Pradesh
(Photo: G. Horter)
Frontispiece: Konyak Nagas breaking through the
forest during a head-hunting ritual
(Photo: P. Nalin)
Endpapers: Traditional Ao-Naga warrior shawl

Edited by Michele Schons

Library of Congress Card Number: 00-104163

Photographic Credits: see p. 168

Prestel books are available worldwide.
Visit our website www.prestel.com
or contact one of the following
Prestel offices for further information:

Head Office: Mandlstrasse 26 · 80802 Munich
Tel. +49 (089) 381709-0, Fax +49 (089) 381709-35
e-mail: sales@prestel.de
Prestel London: 4 Bloomsbury Place · London WC1A 2QA
Tel. +44 (020) 7323 5004, Fax +44 (020) 7636 8004
e-mail: sales@prestel-uk.co.uk
Prestel New York: 175 Fifth Avenue, Suite 402, New York, NY 10010
Tel. +1 (212) 995 27 20, Fax +1 (212) 995 2733
e-mail: sales@prestel-usa.com

First published in India by
Mapin Publishing
31 Somnath Road
Usmanpura
Ahmedabad 380013
Tel: 91-79-755-1833
Fax: 91-79-755-0955
e-mail: mapinpub@vsnl.com
www.mapinpub.com

Map p. 6 by Anneli Nau, Munich
Designed and typeset by Iris von Hoesslin, Munich
Layout by Peter van Ham
Lithography by Eurocrom 4, Villorba
Printed by Pera Druck, Gräfelfing
Bound by Almesberger, St. Georgen im Attg.

Printed in Germany on acid-free paper

ISBN 3-7913-2399-7 (Prestel)
ISBN 81-85822-77-8 (Mapin)

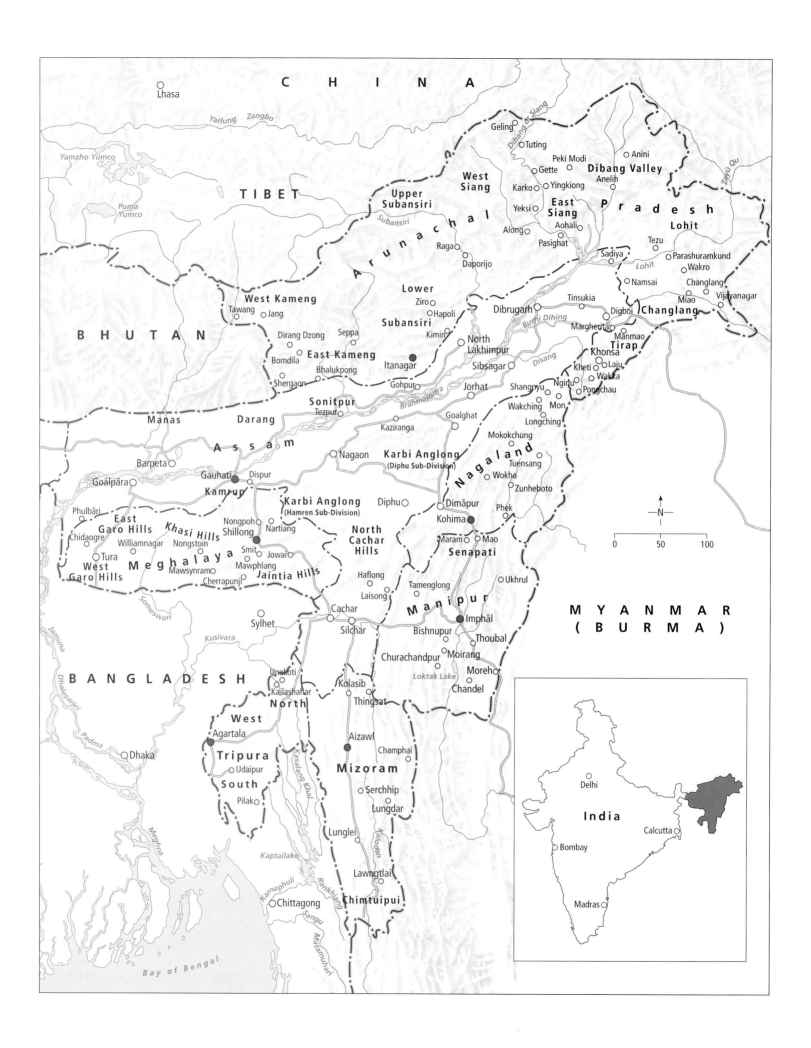

PREFACE

I am alarmed when I see – not only in this country but in other great countries too – how anxious people are to shape others according to their own image or likeness, and to impose on them their particular way of living. This applies equally to national and international fields.
We are welcome to our way of living, but why impose it on others? In fact there would be more peace in the world if people were to desist from imposing their way of living on other people and countries. I am not at all sure which is the better way of living, the tribal or our own. In some respects I am quite certain theirs is better. Therefore, it is grossly presumptuous on our part to approach them with an air of superiority, to tell them how to behave or what to do and what not to do. There is no point in trying to make them a second rate copy of ·
ourselves.   Jawaharlal Nehru

Without the help of numerous friends and well-wishers this book would not have been possible. We are deeply indebted to all of the following:
The India Tourist Office, Frankfurt am Main, Germany—P.K. Dong, S. Sharma, Alok Chowdhury and Mashanta Romani, for their support and excellent travel arrangements; the Indian Consulate General, Frankfurt am Main, Germany—Prabha Murthi and Asha Shrivastava, for arranging special permits. This was facilitated by letters of reference from P.K. Dong, Monika Thaler, Jürgen Tesch and Bipin

India and its north-eastern states, the "Seven Sisters".

Shah. Thanks are also due to the directors and staff of the Tourist Offices in Tripura, Mizoram, Assam and Calcutta, who understood our goals perfectly and helped us to the best of their possibilities. Our 1998 journey was only made possible through the dedicated help of Donyi Hango Tours, Naharlagun, Arunachal Pradesh. We are most indebted to Yane and Ozing Dai and their families as well as to T. Lowang Rajkumar, Minister of Arunachal Pradesh, his brother Manwang and his wife Shampa for their fantastic organization, for opening up their world for us and for becoming great friends along the way. For their company in 1996, we would like to thank Detlev Schwarz and Dr. Angelika Stirn, who has remained helpful and supportive over the years.
For letting us in on many of the secrets of Northeast India we would like to thank: Mokar Riba, Itanagar, T. Tongluk, Khonsa, Lhundup Choesang and the monks of Tawang monastery, as well as Tsering Lama and the members of his cultural group, N. Diwakar, R.C., and K.R. Meena, D.C. of Tirap—for the Govt. of Arunachal Pradesh; Gautam Thokchom, Asha Sinha, Ashu Thokchom and all members of their families, Yambem Laba, H. Jel. Shyam, C.S., and Bharat Singh, Secretary to the Govt. of Manipur, Hadbam Sukumar, Rajesh Salam, Mutua Bahadur, R.S. Yumnam, the "Progressive Artist Laboratory," Smt. Elam Indira Devi and the "Jawaharlal Nehru Manipur Dance Academy," Meisnam Keinahan Devi, N. Harimati Devi and Lokendro Salam (Manipur); Ashok and Nakul Elwin, Bobby D. Majaw, Nesfield Sangma, the Venerable Syiem Sad and her brother A.D. Diengdoh, the members of

the Synkhong Rympai Thymmai, Lumtimai Syemlieh and her mother, Jamon Lang Syemlieh, and her father, Meesha Myrthong, as well as Somu John and James Perry of Cultural Pursuits, Shillong (Meghalaya); the Choudhuri-Mogh family, Rupaichari (Tripura) and all the wonderful villagers of all the different peoples of the "Seven Sisters" who received us with amiable and boundless hospitality and friendliness.
The comprehensive nature of the documentation could only have been achieved through the help and shared knowledge of Prof. Lorenz G. Löffler, Aldesago, Georges Breguet, Geneva, Prof. E. Kausen, Lollar, and through extensive talks with—and with the photographs of—Ashok Diwali, Ashok Nath, Hemen Sanghvi, Gerhard Horter, Günter Gessinger, Axel Gomille, Claus-Dieter Brauns, Patrick Bernard, Thomas Ernsting, L. Dai and K. Chakraborty of the Dept. of Information and Public Relations, the Govt. of Arunachal Pradesh, as well as the Govt. of India Tourist Offices. A special thank you to Pan Nalin, for his considerable help and for entrusting us with so many of his exceptional pictures. A heartfelt thank you to Daniel Oschatz and the team of "Oschatz Visual Media," Wiesbaden, for their support on the photographic front, as well as to Holger Lindner and Bernd van Ham for 'Mac-aid.' A special thank you to Dagmar Schabarum for her intensive work during the writing period, and finally to Prof. G. Overbeck for always doing everything necessary to make our journeys possible.
Dedicated to Dshamilja Ajilamu with deep love and high hopes.

HIDDEN WORLDS BETWEEN TIBET AND BURMA

AN INTRODUCTION

Of all endangered species in the world the indigenous peoples are the most important ones – not because they are human, but because it is only them, who may show the "civilized" that there is no way of life, which may exclusively be called "right"... (D. Quinn) [1]

To write a book on the worlds lying between Tibet and Burma, in India's wild Northeast, is not an easy task. What is to be illustrated seems too complex and too multifaceted, the cultures too diverse, and the untouched nature of the area too unique. To attempt such an undertaking, nevertheless, arises from the desire to acknowledge the fascinating people of this unknown part of the earth. For us, this desire derived from what we were fortunate to experience in the regions of Northeast India, and what we witnessed there. After having to wait ten years for government-imposed travel restrictions, which had been in place since the 1950s, to be lifted, we stepped onto Assam's soil for the first time in 1996, from where we moved on to explore the surrounding states. Here we encountered a number of different peoples whose level of human cultural development is equivalent to that of thousands of years ago. Many of these people still live at one with their ancestors, and in their opinion, the jungles surrounding them are

A Tutsa boy in southern Arunachal Pradesh.

inhabited by spirits. They have maintained their belief in the magic qualities of the animals of the forest. Some of the people have remained hunters and collectors to the present day. The region's farmers still work using the simplest means—the wheel or plough has not yet found its way into their daily lives.

Yet their intuitive knowledge about an all-encompassing unity, and their awareness of the danger of drifting away from this, while still being able to redress the balance, are concepts that continue to occupy an important place in their lives. Their life cycle is strongly ritualized. They pray, dance and make sacrifices for the fertility of their fields, and acknowledge the ancient forces of the earth, sky, water, wind and stars. Close proximity to these forces is maintained through daily rituals and their benefits utilized as much as possible. These people are very conscious of the danger of losing this age-old wisdom by turning to a westernized lifestyle, which has recently pervaded the Northeast, and which, inevitably, has had a strong impact on them.

Our book is dedicated to this hard struggle to hold back such changes. Following the wish explicit of the people we met on our journeys, we have documented the unique qualities of these cultures—in order to preserve them, as they have themselves said, for their own posterity.

A first attempt to present a comprehensive picture of the entire region of the Northeast in photographs and text, cannot

possibly document all aspects. The sheer number of the different groups—almost 500—prevents that. Therefore we have tried to compile an overview of those subjects that best describe those elements that the traditional cultures of these people have in common, while still highlighting their unique customs. We are aware of the fact that some of the traditions we describe, such as head-hunting or animal sacrifice, may seem primitive, barbaric or even offensive to a westerner. But it is not for us to judge the people of this region. As the great anthropologist Verrier Elwin put it: *"So-called civilized countries, which can destroy whole populations with a single atom bomb, can hardly afford to look down on a method of ritual warfare which, at the most, involved the loss of a few hundred lives every year."* [2] In connection with this introduction's initial quotation, we therefore merely describe age-old customs, and their background concepts, knowing that this is what makes the people of the Northeast so special, while being aware that technical developments are taking place in this area of India and do have an enormous impact on the lifestyle of the people. Whether this is positive or negative, only the future will tell.

THE SEVEN SISTERS OF INDIA

THE TRIBAL REALM

This land is not like our land,
its sky is not like our sky.
Its sky sends rain down without the
originating cause of clouds;
On its ground the green grass sprouts
up without any aid from the soil.
It stands outside the circle of the Earth
and the bowels of the enveloping
Sphere.
The seasons all begin here at the time of
their conclusion elsewhere.
Here there is heat in our winter and chill
in our summer.
Its roads are frightful as the path leading
to the Nook of Death;
Fatal to life is its expense like the
unpeopled City of Destruction.
Its forests are full of violence like the
heart of the ignorant.
Its rivers are beyond limit and estimate
like the minds of the wise . . .[1]

Thus the Mulla Darvish of Herat, author of
the *Raja of Assam*, eloquently described his
impressions of the forests along the
northeastern border of India, during a
campaign some 300 years ago. Although
much of this vast region, which, only 50
years ago, had been almost completely

The West Kameng District of Arunachal Pradesh
encompasses an area referred to as the "fog hole," so
called because of its dense rainforests, which release
massive amounts of moisture. In clear weather the
countryside reveals its unique and stunning beauty.

isolated and unexplored and went by the
name of "Assam," is more readily accessible
today than in Darvish's time, his lyrical
descriptions have not lost their relevance.
Still mysterious, fierce and almost immeasu-
rably vast are the modern states of
Arunachal Pradesh, Nagaland, Manipur,
Mizoram, Tripura, Meghalaya and Assam,
which constitute the "Seven Sisters." (In
1999 the Central Government declared the
state of Sikkim, located north of West
Bengal, between Eastern Nepal and Bhutan,
the eighth state of the Northeast, although
culturally it differs considerably from the
other states of the region.) Until recently
their melodic names have failed to evoke
many associations, either geographical or
cultural. Perhaps Assam is best known for
its tea, its Indian rhinos, its flooding and its
political problems . . . But what about the
other states?

Politically they are part of India. Together
they form a triangle of sorts, which
constitutes India's Northeast, otherwise
known as the "Seven Sisters of India."
Framed by Tibet in the north, China in the
east, Burma in the south and Bangladesh in
the west, the region's appellation is apt, for
it evokes associations with the motherland,
India, and, at the same time, a sense of
separateness.

The Northeast of India is a region of
great natural and cultural diversity. From the
icy Himalayan peaks, which culminate in
Mount Kangto (7,090 m) in the Western
Kameng District of Arunachal Pradesh, to

the humid plains of Assam and Tripura,
Northeast India is home to almost every
climatic zone on earth. Only deserts are not
to be found in this area, which belongs to
one of the wettest regions in the world. The
"Seven Sisters of India" consist almost
entirely of hilly, forested terrain formed by
the collision of the Indian Subcontinent with
the Central Asian Plateau. The Himalayas
find their final eastern limit in the state of
Mizoram, in countless mountain ranges that
extend in a northeast-southwest direction.
The region is interspersed with deep gorges
and numerous rivers rich in fish. One of
Asia's mightiest rivers, the Brahmaputra,
penetrates the Himalayas at the Indo-
Tibetan border, between the Namcha Barwa
and Gyala Peri mountains, in the
inaccessible and unexplored Siang Gorge,
which winds its way through Arunachal
Pradesh, in a district of the same name,
before reaching Assam.

A wide variety of plant and animal life
has been able to survive in the region's
untouched rainforests, primarily in
Arunachal Pradesh, such as the takin
(*Budorcas taxicolor*), which is endemic to
Northeast India, and eastern Bhutan, the
mithan buffalo (*Bos frontalis*) and the
hoolock gibbon (*Hylobates hoolock*). Several
expedition parties ventured to Arunachal
Pradesh as late as the 1950s in search of a
fabled animal called the "Buru," which is
said to roam the rainforests of the Subansiri
District.[2] Thirty-two territories in Northeast
India have been declared nature preserves

From top left to bottom right:
Lake Umiam, Meghalaya, near the state's capital, Shillong.

Many small rivers and brooks crisscross the hills of Mizoram (Champhai District).

The entire state of Manipur is hilly and inhabited by several Naga tribes. Shown here are the Kabui Hills, which stretch from southern Assam (Silchar) to Imphal, the state capital.

The southern district of Tripura is particularly fertile.

Vast stretches of virgin rainforest cover many parts of Arunachal Pradesh (Subansiri District).

and national parks, the most famous of which is Kaziranga National Park in Assam, with its large populations of Indian rhinos and tigers, both endangered species. Keibul Lamjao National Park is located in Manipur and encompasses Lake Loktak. Its floating islands are the natural habitat of one of the most endangered species in the world: the Sangai, or brow-antlered deer (*Cervus eldi eldi*). The forests of this state are also home to a multitude of rare medicinal plants, and the Sirhoi lily (*Lilium mackliniae*), which grows exclusively in the Ukhrul District of Manipur.[3] Moreover, more than 500 orchid species have been recorded in Arunachal Pradesh.

One of the wettest regions on earth, Northeast India is where two monsoons spill their contents every year. The Lohit District of Arunachal Pradesh boasts a yearly rainfall of 12,000 mm per square meter. For many years the town of Cherrapunjee in Meghalaya held the world record in annual precipitation, with 22,987 mm per annum; today the record is held by the town of Mawsynram, 10 km from Cherrapunjee, with 12,163 mm per annum. It is no wonder, then, that the windswept highlands of Meghalaya are sometimes called the "Scotland of the East."[4] Such high rainfalls cause the great rivers of Northeast India to swell to alarming degrees every year and are largely responsible for the annual floods in Bangladesh. Although one might think that the rains ensure bountiful harvests, arable soil is found only in several of the lower regions of Assam and Tripura, for the soil of the rainforests and mountain regions is by and large infertile.

In addition to its exuberant beauty and wealth of rare flora and fauna Northeast India's uniqueness lies in the ethnic diversity of its inhabitants, who, like those of the Amazon Basin, have been able to preserve their cultural identity under the sheltering roof of the rainforest or in lofty and impenetrable mountain realms. The cultures that have developed in this vast area have little in common with what is considered "typically Indian." The majority of the

From top to bottom: *Examples of the extraordinarily rich rice dishes of the Tripuran Mogh cuisine.*
Tea pickers in Assam, which supplies one-third of the world's tea.
Crossing the Burmese border in Mizoram.
The plains of Tripura are used for extensive rubber plantations.

population living here is not of Indo-Aryan stock but descends from those who migrated here centuries ago from Mongolia, Tibet, China, Burma, Laos, Cambodia and Thailand. They practice their own, mostly animistic-shamanistic or polytheistic, religions, and their attitudes and life-styles vary greatly from those of Central Indians. Culturally unique they have formed strong interracial bonds, often obscuring the already complex tribal relations. The clan and the family preside over society. Unusual forms of society, such as matrilineal descent, have survived here, as well as life in long-houses, ritual tattooing, animal sacrifices and cults surrounding the custom of head-hunting.

Owing to the remoteness of the region, the support given to the "Seven Sisters" by the Central Government has been difficult to put into effect. The tasks of establishing a communication network and of stimulating economic growth and educational development have proven difficult. On the other hand, corruption and mismanagement also prevent the region from flourishing. During British colonial rule such efforts had failed primarily because of the resistance put up by the native peoples, who defended their territory, sometimes even with weapons. Initially the British reacted with merciless destruction. More often than not, however, they retreated as quickly as they came and were content to keep their administrative officials in safe areas, away from the malaria-infested jungles.

After India gained independence in 1947 the Northeast began to receive more attention. Owing to the political developments in southern Asia following World War II—such as the end of English colonial rule in Burma and India, the formation of a communist regime in Burma, the expansion of communist China into Tibet and present-day Arunachal Pradesh and the establishment of Western and Eastern Pakistan—it became increasingly necessary for fledgling India to explore its border regions and to secure its international borders, a process requiring the development of communication and road networks, for military purposes if nothing else.

Thus, did the people of the Northeast Indian states step out of their isolation. Their reactions to being "discovered" varied. Initial contact was established in the 1950s by such unescorted government officials as anthropologists J. P. Mills,[5] Verrier Elwin[6] and Christoph von Fürer-Haimendorf[7]

The Sirhoi lily is endemic to the Sirhoi Valley, Ukhrul District, eastern Manipur.

Right: Much like neighboring Bangladesh, most of Tripura is at a relatively low elevation and therefore boasts an abundance of water, which is necessary for large-scale rice cultivation.

On an island in Lake Rudrasagar, the late ruler of Tripura had Neermahal Palace built, which can still be reached only by boat.

and was, by and large, amicable. The scientists supplied information to the Central Government about the inhabitants of the region. Increasing pressure was exerted on Delhi to see to the needs of the peoples of the Northeast—even if they were not part of mainstream Indian society—to respect them and to include them in the decision-making process involved in developing the border regions.

The people's attitude toward this inclusion was twofold: on the one hand they welcomed it in the hope of improving their standard of living, on the other hand they felt in no way connected to mainland India. Many wanted to be independent and left to their own devices. But India was by no means willing to keep its enormous border area unmonitored and inaccessible, leaving it open to foreign influence. Therefore, in the 1960s, India began to divide its northeastern territories into separate states. Compared to Tripura and Manipur, which had been small Hindu kingdoms and proved to be least opposed to becoming Indian states, the ethnic diversity of Assam, with its Nagas, Kukis, Chins, Shans and other Tibeto-Burmese peoples, forced mainland India to divide up this vast area according to ethnographic considerations in order to stifle the hostility among the various tribes, which at that time were striving for independence.

Yet, in the eyes of certain political groups of Nagaland, Manipur, Tripura, Mizoram and Assam, India was only partly successful, which caused political unrest in nearly all the states of Northeast India and continues to make itself felt today. Some states even harbor underground activists who employ militant means to achieve their goals, such as the independence of a particular ethnic group and the territorial demarcation accompanying it, enforced financial remittance or the appointment of native peoples in the administration, which is otherwise dominated by mainland Indians. An additional problem is the open hostility shown to refugees posted in Northeast India, mainly from Bangladesh, whose number in Arunachal Pradesh alone is estimated to be between 40,000 and 60,000. This attitude has to do with the way the native peoples view themselves, which has always been bound up with a particular territory. Those who penetrate this territory have always been regarded as natural enemies by the inhabitants. This attitude has been the source of innumerable interethnic disputes, which, for the outsider, are nearly incomprehensible. They have existed since ancient times and, as the efforts of the Central Government to find solutions to the problems by means of diplomacy have proven, are seemingly unresolvable in some instances.[8]

It is mainly owing to this internal unrest that Northeast India has, until recently, remained a "terra incognita" to foreign visitors. In 1995 the Ministry of Internal Affairs loosened travel restrictions, opening up to visitors traveling in groups certain routes through the "Seven Sisters" region, a land of unfathomable beauty and great cultural diversity.

Opposite, top left: *Many parts of Arunachal Pradesh are still accessible only on foot via dangerous paths and cane bridges, such as this one at Peki Modi, upper Siang. Photograph: G. Horter.*

Opposite, bottom left: *A sign in Itanagar, the capital of Arunachal Pradesh, revealing the open hostility shown to refugees.*

Opposite, right: *The hilly terrain of Arunachal Pradesh prohibits large-scale woodcutting. In many parts of the country, where machines are of no use, elephants provide the only help available.*

Right: *In some parts of Northeast India, particularly in the remote border regions, opium poppy is cultivated—another factor that has contributed to the strained relationship between the indigenous peoples and the Central Government. Traditionally the dried juice of the opium poppy was used to cure malaria and illnesses affecting the gastrointestinal tract. Smoked in so-called* Kanigun *pipes the drug offers fast pain relief but at the high price of rapid addiction. Curiously the addiction rate varies from tribe to tribe. It is very high among the Mishmis, who grow the plant extensively in the lower regions of the Siang District, relatively high among the Konyak Nagas, the Noctes and the Wanchos and unknown among the Adis, who grow opium poppy in upper Siang. An explanation for this might be the strong sense of social responsibility encountered among the Adis, whose environmental and social consciousness has enabled them to preserve both the environment and their ancient traditions.*

Top left: *Two Bori-Adi boys from Arunachal's remotest district, upper Siang.*

Bottom left: *In the early days of exploration in the region the Gallong-Adis, then known as Abors ("wild men"), were fierce and hostile.*

Top right: *The isolation of Northeast India, especially the rainforests of Arunachal Pradesh, has led to the preservation of a rich and unique cultural heritage, as reflected in the peoples' clothing, customs, language, religion, etc. Gallong-Adis performing the Ponung dance during the Mopin festival. The miri, or chant leader, recounts the genealogy of the*
Gallongs and the girl dancers respond by repeating the verses.

Bottom right: *The Adis have preserved their traditional village councils, kebangs, and the Indian Central Government has kept local jurisprudence in the hands of these age-old institutions—one of the reasons why many of the tribal societies of Arunachal Pradesh are in the fortunate position of being able to preserve their cultural heritage with dignity and pride, without losing touch with modern developments.*

Top left: The jewelry of this Aka chief reveals the proximity of his territory to Tibet: silver, coral and a ga'u, an amulet box in the shape of a vajra, the Tibetan thunderbolt, adorn his ears and neck.
Top and bottom right: Minyong- and Gallong-Adi hunters decorated with boars' tusks, tiger jaws, bear furs, monkey tails and hornbill beaks.

The tradition of head-hunting among the Naga
peoples of Nagaland, Manipur and Arunachal
Pradesh made the exploration of these territories
extremely dangerous. Opposite: A Nishi hunter of
Arunachal's Subansiri District, wearing his hunting
attire made from nettle fiber and a cane hat
adorned with feathers, beak, and the claws of a

THE INDIGENOUS PEOPLES OF NORTHEAST INDIA AND THEIR ORIGINS

All human beings are the children of Father Heaven and Mother Earth. A long time ago they descended from the heavens on ladders. Each race had its own ladder assigned to it. According to their status they were either of gold, silver, iron or simply bamboo or grass. (Aka creation myth)[1]

Twenty-eight main ethnic groups, of which 110 subgroups exist, inhabit Arunachal Pradesh; 78 live in India's second smallest state, Tripura; 23 in Meghalaya; 25 in Nagaland; 17 in Mizoram; 13 in Manipur; and more than 20 in Assam—an overwhelming and almost inconceivable ethnic diversity in an area covering approximately 250,000 sq. km. Some 35 million people live in this region, in varying degrees of density, ranging from overpopulated Assam and Tripura, bordering on Bangladesh, to the solitary giant of Arunachal Pradesh, in which there are only 10 inhabitants per square kilometer.[2]

Northeast India represents a sort of ethnological transition zone between India and neighboring China, Tibet, Burma and Bangladesh. Yet the ancestors of many ethnic groups living here hailed from far, further-flung regions, as may be surmised from the languages spoken and the creation myths of the tribes living here. It is

A Reang woman from Tripura wearing traditional silver jewelry.

conceivable that the peoples who settled in the area came during the great migrations, some 3,000 years ago.

Situated some distance from the present-day territory of Mizoram, is the homeland of the some 40 clans that, collectively, are called the Mizos (*Mi-zo*—"highlanders"), among which the Lushais, the Hmars, the Raltes, the Paites and the Zos are the most numerous. Their ancestors seem to have migrated from the Tao Valley in north-western China's Kansu Province. Prince Chin Lung, son of Shin Huang-ti, emperor of the Ch'in Dynasty in the seventh century A.D., who was responsible for the initial construction of the Great Wall of China, was forced to leave his homeland, together with his following, on account of a dispute he had with his father. Over the centuries his people migrated via central Burma to the extreme north of modern-day Mizoram, into the Chin and Mizo Hills.[3]

The Naga tribes of Nagaland (Burmese: *Na-Ka*—"people with pierced earlobes"; Assamese: *Noga*—"naked") and Manipur are most likely of Southeast Asian or even Oceanic origin. Thus one finds strong cultural affinities with Malaysian and Indonesian peoples. Some anthropologists even believe that because of their similar appearance, some Naga groups are related to the peoples of Papua New Guinea and Melanesia. The route taken by the various Naga tribes cannot be traced. It is therefore impossible to ascertain whether they ventured northward from Indonesia or

whether they parted ways in present-day Nagaland. The dialects of the Nagas, which vary from village to village, form a separate group in the Tibeto-Burman language family and reveal certain affinities with the Sino-Tibetan and Burmese languages.

The Nagas of Nagaland are composed of 15 different subtribes, which go by the melodic names of Angami, Ao, Chakesang, Chang, Kabui, Khiamniungam, Konyak, Lotha, Phom, Pochury, Rengma, Sangtam, Sema, Yimchunger and Zeliang. Their territory extends into Arunachal Pradesh and Burma. The Nagas living in the mountainous regions of Manipur include the Chiru Marrings, the Kabuis, the Khoiraos, the Kolyas, the Maos, the Maram Mayangs, the Quoirengs, the Tangkhuls and the Zemis.

The Meitheis represent the dominant population in Manipur, and inhabit the valley in which the capital, Imphal, is situated. Indo-Aryan, Burmese, Thai and Chinese features may be discerned in their faces. Additionally an influence of southern India can be traced to several words in the Meithei language that derive from Dravidian Tamil.[4]

Equally diverse are the facial features of the Khasis in Meghalaya, who bear a closer resemblance to the Thai, the Cambodians and the Laotians than to any other ethnic group in Asia. The Khasi language belongs to the Austroasiatic language family and betrays affinities with Burmese Mon and Khmer, which is spoken by the majority of Cambodia's population. Curiously enough

Above: *The dominant population of Manipur, the Meitheis, inhabits the Imphal Valley. Top and bottom, left: Children of the matrilineal Khasis who live in the Khasi Hills of Meghalaya. Opposite top*

left and right: *The Garos live in western Meghalaya, in the east and west Garo Hills. They, too, are a matrilineal people and live in longhouses. Most of them have not been Christianized.*

one even encounters Mongolian words in the Khasi language, such as the salute *kublai*, which goes back to the Great Khan, emperor of the Mongol Dynasty in the 13th century, in the time of Marco Polo, whose name was used as a password throughout the giant kingdom. The other two tribes, perhaps Meghalaya's original inhabitants, are the Garos and the Jaintias. In ancient times their settlements were strictly separated from each other by the deep gorges of the state's mountainous regions. Even today the only place where one finds all three groups living in close proximity to each other is around the capital, Shillong.[5]

The peoples of Arunachal Pradesh can be divided into several main groups. According to the latest census, in 1981, the 15 different animistic Adi peoples of the Subansiri and Siang Districts, of which many belong to 30 subclans, predominate, with 121,000 people, and are most influential culturally. They are followed by 91,000 of the Nishi-Bangni-Sulung group. Comparable in number are the six Lamaistic main groups of the Monpa (35,000) in the Kameng and

Tawang Districts, near the borders of Bhutan and Tibet, and the 33,000 of the Wancho group living in the Tirap District, followed by 25,000 members of the three main Mishmi tribes inhabiting the mountainous and wooded Lohit District as well as the 15 different Tangsa groups of the Changlang and Tirap Districts (17,000). Twenty-four smaller ethnic groups make up the rest of Arunachal's diverse population, of which the Aka-Miji-Khowa group, the Apa Tanis and the Noctes are of unique cultural and anthropological interest. Three further groups continue to migrate to Arunachal Pradesh. Forty-two different languages are spoken in the "Land of the Rising Sun," mostly of Sino-Tibetan origin; six written languages are in use.[6]

As diverse as the languages in Arunachal are the different theories as to their origin, which rarely help trace the origin of individual tribes. The appearance of the Akas, for example, a small ethnic group in the eastern Kameng District, bears little relation to the language they speak. Their yellow-brown skin, flat faces and almond-shaped eyes are typical Mongolian features; however, their language is associated with the Burmese Shan dialects, as they are spoken south of the Patkoi Mountains.[7]

The various racial groups of Assam also exhibit a wide range of facial features, many of which would support the hypothesis that they migrated from the northwest (India, Tibet, China) and southeast (Burma, Cambodia). Along the valleys of the Brahmaputra and Bharak Rivers live primarily Hindu and Muslim groups, as well as a few practicing Buddhists (Aitons, Doanias, Tai Phakes, Turungs). The originally animistic Boros— which include the Boro and Sonowal Cacharis, the Chutiyas, the Lalungs and the Rabhas (associated with the Bodo subgroup of the Tibeto-Burmese) as well as some of the Mishings, who migrated from Arunachal Pradesh—have adopted these religions, retaining only a few of their ancient traditions. However the Karbis and the Dimasas, who reside in the mountainous regions of Assam—the districts of Karbi Anglong and north Cachar—have eschewed the religious influence of India. They are composed of 40 patrilineal and 42 matrilineal clans belonging to 12 different religious communities, each headed by their own chief (jamthai). Assam experienced its cultural peak during the reign of the Tai Ahom kings, descendants of the Shan, who hailed from Burma and settled in the Brahmaputra Valley in the 13th century. For nearly 600 years they ruled the country from Sibsagar, located on the southeast bank of the river.[8]

In Tripura, the second smallest state in India after Goa, 23 different languages are spoken. The name of the state derives from the Tripuri, which signifies "children of the water goddess," the largest group among the native inhabitants. The Reangs, the Jamatias, the Noatias and the Halams, with their 12 subtribes, are included in this group. Their dialects belong to the Tibeto-Burman language family. The rest of Tripura's population consists of migrated peoples, whose descendants originated from such neighboring countries as Bangladesh and Burma (e.g., the Buddhist Moghs, the Kukis and the Chakmas from the Chittagong Hills in Bangladesh).[9]

Right: *The Tagins, Nishis, Hill Miris and Apa Tanis belong to the same ethnic group and inhabit the Subansiri District of Arunachal Pradesh.* Photograph left: G. Horter.

Top: *The mandala-shaped foundations of an Orissan-style temple, built between the 14th and 15th centuries, in Malinithan near Likabali in the West Siang District of Arunachal Pradesh.*
Bottom: *Some of the phallic stone monoliths of the Assamese Cachari in Dimapur, Nagaland.*
Photograph: H. Sanghvi.

Archaeological evidence of the ancient inhabitants of Northeast India is scarce. Foundations of temples in the states that are predominated by tribal societies, such as Arunachal Pradesh and Nagaland, go back to the Hindu cultures of the lowlands of Assam and Orissa and are encountered exclusively in the lower border regions (e.g., the 13th-century forts of Bhalukpong in the Kameng and southern Subansiri Districts of Arunachal, the 14th- and 15th-century, Orissan-style Malinithan temples near Likabali in the West Siang District of the same state[10] and the 14th-century Assamese Cachari ruins of Dimapur in Nagaland[11]). The only possible exceptions are the Unakoti engravings in Tripura, which date from between the 11th and 15th centuries and recall the art of the Nagas (see chapter titled "Fertility through Stones and Heads").[12]

Several peoples of Northeast India who maintained contact with Indo-Aryans are mentioned in the epic poems of India. The *Mahabharata*, for instance, contains references to Tripura, one of the oldest kingdoms in India;[13] Assam temples connected with the Tantric Hindu cults; the sacred Parashuram Lake north of Tezu in the Lohit District of Arunachal,[14] whose waters are described as being as sacred as those of the Ganges;[15] and some of the Tibeto-Burmese peoples, called Kiratas, a name used for all non-Indo-Aryan peoples in the Indian epics. Yet these clues do not help identify the origin of hundreds of different peoples. One oddity in the historical evaluation of Northeast India is Ptolemy's mention of the Nagas in his *Geography*, written in the second century A.D.! His description of the Bay of Bengal is inaccurate, but the location he gives for the Naga country, which he calls the "realm of the naked," is correct. Later the Nagas are mentioned once again, in the 13th-century chronicles of the Assamese Ahom kings.[16]

Of considerably greater interest and, in certain respects, much more revealing of the way the peoples of Northeast India view themselves, is their rich mythological heritage, in which the genesis of the various tribes is described. Since the indigenous peoples do not have a written language, their mythology has been transmitted orally over the centuries, from generation to generation and, today, is as alive as ever. As in other cultures many of the attitudes of the peoples as well as their social behaviors can be traced back to the self-

understanding revealed therein. As diverse as these myths are, they reveal striking similarities with regard to man's relationship to nature. The indigenous population does not regard man as being superior to nature. On the contrary, the animals with which man is surrounded are frequently depicted as being more clever, wiser and powerful than man. Like gods and spirits they are thought to have magical powers, with which they can help or harm man. As man does not possess these powers he must rely on the animals' goodwill. In many of the myths man needs time to comprehend this fact. In others man is portrayed as being false and as taking advantage of the goodwill of the animals, thereby excluding himself from the unity of all living things.[17]

The Cachari-Bodos from Assam recount:
In the beginning there was only a deep silence, whence man and woman originated. They were united and the woman became pregnant. In the course of time she laid seven eggs. Out of the first six eggs kings, people and gods slipped, out of the seventh, however, crept the hideous, evil demons that bring disease to man.[18]

In this story, which is also the creation myth of the Singphos—a Buddhist group in the Changlang and Lohit Districts of Arunachal Pradesh who believe that their forebears slipped from the sixth of the seven eggs— no account is given of gods having been the first inhabitants of the world but only of man and woman, perhaps representing duality. Their consummation is not brought about by themselves alone but by some higher power. The myth embraces the notion that all that is divided ultimately strives to be reunited and heeds a higher, unconscious power. Only by uniting opposites does the multifariousness of life unfold. One "Black Jack," or foul egg, is associated with the magic number seven— various forms of illness, which continuously remind man of his mortality and inadequacy. It is interesting to note that the illnesses are portrayed as self-sufficient beings. Such is the case in many animistic-shamanistic traditions. The story reveals the teller's strong sense of self but also his experience of life: all stand on equal ground— men, kings, gods and diseases. Man is viewed as having the potential to become king- or even godlike. Illnesses are not necessarily fatal, for there are often ways to treat them. This can be seen in the rich healing traditions of the indigenous peoples. For many inhabitants of Northeast India the egg, even today, is one of the most important objects used in sacrificial ceremonies and rituals connected with divination—perhaps symbolic of the return to the nonmaterial world, in which the limitations of space and time do not exist.

In their ancestral mythology the Akas from West Kameng District in Arunachal claim to belong to the ruling class:

All human beings are the children of Father Heaven and Mother Earth. A long time ago they descended from the heavens by ladders. Each race had its own ladder assigned to them: the Ahom kings and the Akas of Royal descent came by golden ladders, all other Akas by silver ladders. The Tibetans and Monpas were handed iron ladders, the Nishis and Adis had to be content with bamboo, whereas the Cacharis and the Khowas even had to descend via grass ladders.[19]

This elitist view pervades the attitudes of the Akas toward neighboring tribes. It must be remembered that the Ahom kings, to whom the Akas liken themselves in their mythology, turned Assam into a flourishing kingdom in the 13th century, erected magnificent temples in their capital, Sibsagar, and employed a highly sophisticated written language. Thus, such a comparison does indeed seem rather pretentious. Yet, compared to their neighbors, the Akas do occupy a high place in society. The "barbarians" whom the Akas impute with a lower status either do not live nearby (Nishis, Adis) or they work as servants in Aka society (Khowas).

The mythology of the Morang-Tangsas, who call themselves Mungray (*mung*— "group of humans"; *ray*—"ladder"), also includes a ladder. They believe that, in former times, they lived with God in heaven, but then they were sent to earth. With a ladder they tried to return to heaven, which proved unsuccessful. Ever since they have been waiting for God to send for them.[20] The Khasis of Meghalaya believe that a ladder once connected heaven and earth; however, they take the blame for its disappearance (see chapter titled "Women's Mysterious Realm"). Impressive evidence of the notion of a ladder connecting heaven and earth is the 6-m-high monolith in the Champhai District of Mizoram, which, throughout the region, is referred to as "heaven's ladder."

According to the creation myth of the Mizos, they originated from a cave, from which one clan leader after the next is said to have emerged with their wives. When the first-born of the Ralte subclan appeared, the clan members shouted out with joy, causing the guardian deity of the cave to become frightened and to conclude that the human population had grown too large. He therefore sealed the cave with a stone, preventing more human beings issuing from it.[21] The Angami-, Sema-, Ao- and other Naga peoples claim that they originate from the "bowels of the earth."[22] Both concepts (cave and bowels = opening = vagina and womb) may be interpreted as evidence of the belief in a mother goddess as creator and in femininity as the principal force of creation.

The creation myth of the Nishis, who live in the Dafla Mountains of Arunachal's Subansiri District, is somewhat cruder: "We Nishis also received our share of skin, on which was written the wisdom of the world; but we ate it up in hunger, whereas the people of the plains preserved it." Today the Nishis still believe that knowledge is "remembered in the belly" and thus passed from one generation to the next.[23] In their mythology they claim to be a separate tribe and give themselves a lower status than the peoples of the lowlands, such as the Assamese Ahoms. Despite their lower position in the social hierarchy they take great pride in the legend, for in it they act pragmatically, doing the only thing that is wise: to ensure the survival of their tribe in a hostile and dangerous environment.

In the rough creation myths of the various Mishmi peoples who inhabit the eastern border region of Arunachal[24] Amya Khinya, the "wild god," penetrates the womb of the first woman. The child born of that union becomes the "Father of the Idu." The Miju-Mishmis trace the strength of their

The creation myth of the Akas states that they as well as other tribes came from heaven via ladders. Locally referred to as "heaven's ladder," this 6-m-high, damaged stone monolith is located in Mizoram's Champhai District.
Top photograph: A. Nath

The People of Tripura, Mizoram and Assam. Above: A Zemi-Naga in traditional dress in front of the village morung (bachelors' house). The Zemi-Nagas live in the Cachar Mountains on the Assam-Manipur border. Photograph: P. Bernard. Top left: A Thadou-Kuki warrior from Manipur who settled in Tripura. Center left: Mizo youths from Aizawl, Mizoram, singing traditional songs. Bottom left: Molsum-Halam girls from Tripura waiting for a community dance to commence.

Opposite: In historic times the rivers of Northeast India provided the only means by which people could migrate, for dense tropical vegetation covered almost the entire area. Today bamboo is still transported via the waterways between Tripura and Assam.

tribe back to the only man and woman to survive the devastating tempests, conflagrations and deluges of a primal catastrophe. A similar legend of the Muklom-Tangsas in Arunachal's Changlang District tells of the seven primeval fathers of man who emerged from the "thigh mother," the only woman to live through the great snow storm that once befell *Rangthip*, Mother Earth. The Ronrang-Tangsas, on the other hand, trace their ancestry to a man who married the devil's only daughter.[25]

Many of these myths bear witness to the magical properties these peoples attribute to nature. Animals often figure prominently in them. Accordingly the Dirang-Monpas of West Kameng District in Arunachal Pradesh believe that they descend from a monkey. In accordance with Tibetan Buddhism religion a *lama* by the name of Lapan Rinpoche transformed them from monkeys into humans.[26] The Sanke- and Tonglim-Tangsas of Changlang trace their roots to a tangle of worms that crept from the swollen knee of an orphan.[27] The Zemi-Nagas tell an interesting animal story in connection with their territory: "The king of worms went down to the bottom of the ocean and created many images of himself, until the soil had formed. The crow leveled most of it, but when it came down to leveling the mountains too, she got tired. Therefore the plains are flat and the mountains steep and replete with gorges."

Somewhat similar is the myth of the Ao-Nagas, who attribute the creation of the world to their highest god, Lichaba, who first created the plains but got a stomachache when it was time to level Nagaland and, therefore, did not finish his work.[28]

Stones are even claimed to be man's ancestors in the mythology of the "stone-born" Lungchang-Tangsas (*lung*—"stone"; *chang*—"birth"). A myth of the Sangwal-Tangsas draws the following connection:

> *Once a brother and a sister lived together as a couple. The offspring of such a calamitous relationship could never become a child, but only a stone. Angry and disappointed the couple proceeded to set the stone on fire, which splintered into a thousand little pieces. Each piece was one human couple. One of them founded the Sangwal line.*[29]

The creation myth of the Sangwals had clear repercussions for their marriage customs, which, to this day, are among the strictest of all Northeast Indian societies.

Many tribes permit the marriage of cousins, for example, which is prohibited among the Sangwals.

In Tripurean Reang mythology an angel received two stones from God, which he gave to a bird to brood over. Of these stones the first man and woman were born. They were brother and sister. Their incestuous union produces two eggs, from which the heroes of Reang mythology emerge.[30]

Other Northeast Indian societies also believe that they descend from a stone. Six Naga tribes trace their roots to a gigantic stone located in the village of Khezakenoma.[31] The order in which the individual tribes are thought to have emerged from it forms the basis of the position they occupy in the social hierarchy of the Nagas.

Once a year the Zemi-Nagas celebrate their biggest festival—the ritual stone-jump. It evolved from the belief that certain stones (like the ones from which the Nagas are thought to have originated) have the potential to be fertile. Some Naga tribes believe that such stones would appear in a vision to a member of the tribe, such as after a successful head-hunt. These stones were regarded as extremely precious, for they symbolized the potential fertility of their finders. Although head-hunting has been banned in Naga society, the Zemis still jump across their ancient stones, located next to the village morung (bachelors' house), to activate the stones' precious powers.

Opposite: *A Sema-Naga in full attire.*
Photographs: P. Bernard.

In many parts of the Tirap District of Arunachal Pradesh the Wanchos still live very traditionally. In many villages their only dress till the present day consists of a small loin cloth only. The men all have the same significant haircut and blacken their teeth with soot as a way of hygiene and prevention of germs.

Like the Wanchos of Arunachal Pradesh several other groups also belong to the tribal community of the Nagas. Until the state of Arunachal Pradesh was formed the Tuensang district of Nagaland, the territory of the Phom-, Konyak- and Chang-Nagas, temporarily belonged to the "NEFA", India's Northeast frontier agency. Even today the different groups of the Naga liberation movement strive to unite all Naga peoples living in Nagaland, Manipur, Arunachal Pradesh and even Burma. Photographs of Tangkhul and Konyak Nagas: P. Nalin.

3

THE APA TANIS

FATHERS OF MANKIND IN A RICE BOWL

The sight is one I shall never forget, when we suddenly emerged on a magnificent plateau some ten miles in length, laid out in highly cultivated terraces watered by the Kale River. The valley was dotted with isolated hillocks, and low pine-clad spurs ran here and there into the valley from the eastern ranges. Our hearts warmed at the sight of primroses, violets, wild currants, strawberries and raspberries, and I felt disposed almost to believe some of the wonderful stories we had heard of the fabulous wealth of this country.
(McCabe, 1897)[1]

In the misty forests of the Subansiri District of Arunachal Pradesh, encircled by 2,500-m-high mountains, a 26-sq.-km-wide and 1,600-m-high enclave forms the small area in which one of the most remarkable societies of Northeast India resides. This is the home of the Apa Tanis, as they call themselves, the direct descendants of the first man, Abotani. Their valley has left a deep and romantic impression on all explorers who have ventured here. Little has changed over the years on the Apa Tani Plateau, and, despite the natural limitations of the inhabitable space, the Apa Tanis have managed to create a little "economic miracle."

From childhood on Apa Tani women wear giant nose plugs, inserted into their nostrils.

The "rice bowl" of the Apa Tanis is framed by eight villages: Hija, Bela, Hari, Hang, Duta, Bamin, Tage and Hapoli. Owing to the strategic importance of the plateau, the latter town—the southernmost in the valley, was expanded, becoming the new district headquarters of the Indian government and a military base, including an airstrip—and is now called Ziro.

The Apa Tani tribe comprises more than 15,000 souls. A strict social system has ensured their survival in an area restricted to a single valley and in a hostile environment inhabited by the warlike Nishi and Hill Miri tribes. This system is reflected in many facets of Apa Tani cultural and social life. Striking at first is the meticulous division of the land surrounding the fields, which is reserved for housing. The 640 houses of Hija recall modern terraced houses, crowded along a main road. All main roads in the villages terminate in broad squares in which rectangular platforms (*lapangs*) have been erected. These up to 9-m-long and 1.5-m-high stages are places of public gatherings. They attest to the democratic Apa Tani society, which has developed out of necessity. No Apa Tani house is large enough to accommodate a public gathering. The restricted environment prohibits exclusive clan institutions from being developed and leading members of society, such as chiefs, from being granted prerogatives to display publicly their elevated status, in the form of a big house, for example. It would seem that the Apa

Tanis never felt it necessary to grant such special privileges to select people and their families when several families could occupy the same living space.

The main roads branch out from the squares, forming further village quarters, which are designed according to similar principles and are inhabited by different clans. In an Apa Tani town such clan quarters generally constitute separate villages and are regarded as being more or less politically autonomous entities.

Every Apa Tani family owns a small plot of land, usually located at the back of the house in which they live or in designated areas near the forests, where a small selection of vegetables, fruit, pine trees and a particular variety of fast-growing male bamboo are grown. Alone the foresight to grow bamboo and pine trees reveals an astonishing degree of environmental consciousness among the Apa Tanis, which sets them apart from their neighbors, such as the Nishis, who are traditionally mere hunters and gatherers and who practice the primitive slash-and-burn method of cultivation. If the Apa Tanis did not systematically and regularly replant trees the community's firewood supplies would have been depleted long ago. Traveling great distances to find firewood would have proven laborious and inefficient, eventually causing the relocation and dispersion of the various clans. This, in turn, would have weakened the internal cohesion of the community, making it easy prey to hostile neighboring

The skyline of a typical Apa Tani village is marked by bobo poles, reaching up to 18 m in height, which are usually erected around platforms for public gatherings (lapangs). They may have originally symbolized phalluses, for they are built during the annual mloko spring festival, when the community prays for fertility. Long ropes are tied to the tips of the bobo poles, which are bent to and fro by a group of youths until supple. By bending the pole back far enough, an Apa Tani boy, who holds on tightly to the rope, is catapulted into the air. During those few weightless seconds he does acrobatic stunts high above the village roofs and spectators.

tribes. Like the division of the land the well-thought-out reforestation strategy serves to perpetuate the community as a whole. To this day the Apa Tanis trade valuables for a few pine sprouts, if they do not already have some in their own gardens. Planting a pine tree does not serve the generation of the planter or even necessarily that of his children. Yet this is done out of a sense of responsibility toward future generations, who will invariably need the wood to construct new houses. The conservation of natural resources as well as the system of terraced cultivation, which has been used by the Apa Tanis for ages, are cultural achievements that, compared to the destructive slash-and-burn methods employed by most of the Northeast Indian peoples, attest to the Apa Tanis' superior environmental consciousness.

By observing the traditional culture of the Apa Tanis today one can begin to understand how Neolithic societies functioned, which, under more favorable circumstances than those of this isolated Himalayan valley, had developed into the great pre- and protohistoric societies of Asia. This is because the Apa Tanis still have much in common with prehistoric man, making their achievements even more remarkable! As recent as four generations ago the Apa Tanis had never seen metal implements. Inventions such as the plow and the wheel did not reach the Apa Tanis until the mid-19th century. Only when the tea plantations were laid out in Assam in the 1850s did the Apa Tanis become acquainted with iron hoes, which rapidly replaced the traditional digging sticks and buffalo shoulder blades that had previously been used for tilling soil.

The Apa Tanis still till their fields by means of sheer manpower—with the hoe instead of the plow. The reason for this is that the strictly circumscribed terrain prohibits extensive buffalo breeding. Too much fertile soil would have to be used for animal husbandry and too much damage could be done to the fields. In the spring the Apa Tanis are, of course, mainly preoccupied with agricultural tasks. Long before the sun drives away the veils of morning mist, the women set out digging, fertilizing and weeding the dry soil of their private gardens. Shortly after sunrise they return to their houses to prepare breakfast or to do the necessary housework. After-ward they set out again to the rice fields, this time together with their husbands, to sow seeds, water the fields or transplant the cuttings of the seven different types of rice grown here.

The men's tasks include repairing irrigation canals and constructing new dams along the fields, which contiguously span the entire length of the valley. They are watered by a cleverly devised network of irrigation ditches and pipelines and are the source of Apa Tani wealth, which has enabled the inhabitants of this relatively densely populated valley to enjoy a higher

Things change quickly, even in remote Apa Tani society. In these photographs three generations are shown: a 40-year-old woman and her husband (below), their son and grandson.

standard of living than those of most other tribes in this part of the Himalayas. They even produce a surplus of crops frequently, which has led to the development of a fascinating bartering system with neighboring tribes: the Apa Tanis trade their rice and millet for meat, in the form of mithan buffaloes, with the Nishis. Curiously enough mithans serve primarily ritual and cultic purposes in Apa Tani society. Such trading developed out of the necessity to coexist peacefully with the neighboring tribes to ensure their own survival. Nevertheless raids by the hostile Nishis, who envied the Apa Tanis' prosperity, were a routine occurrence until only recently, often seriously endangering the Apa Tani community, especially the women, who have the reputation of being much more beautiful than those of neighboring tribes.

Apa Tani society has always been divided into an upper class, consisting of

landowning aristocracy (called *mites* or *guths*), and a landless lower class comparable in status with serfs (*muras* or *guchis*). However, the relationship between the *mites* and the *muras* has always been marked by social responsibility and, in everyday life, there exists only one uncrossable barrier between the two classes: the marriage law. Yet premarital relations between members of both classes are permitted. A member of the lower class can acquire wealth and status, just as a *mite* can become impoverished. Apa Tani society is comparable with the Indian caste system in that the social, religious and ceremonial life of both are marked by complex interclass relations and mutual dependencies. On the other hand the caste system promises social advancement and change through reincarnation, whereas the Apa Tani's religion does not—evidence that clearly speaks in favor of the latter having been conceived by members of the upper class.

Thus *nelli*, the afterworld, reflects earthly life. In the case of natural death the human soul (*yalo*) is believed to vanish into a subterranean realm that is guarded by *nelkiri*, the guardian spirit who decides the

status the dead person is to enjoy in *nelli*, based on his earthly wealth and merit, such as the number of animals he sacrificed to the gods in his lifetime. The deceased are thought to rejoin their animals and family, as well as any serfs left behind. Every deceased woman is reunited with her first husband in the realm of the dead and people who have died unmarried may marry and bear children in the afterworld. A multitude of gods and spirits (*wiyus*) live in *nelli*. They are trying to possess the souls of the sick or unconscious, which roam around aimlessly and unguarded. If such a soul is captured by a *wiyu* only the shaman is able to make contact with the spirit realm to redeem the victim's soul by offering sacrifices to the *wiyus*. Souls of people having died unnatural or violent deaths enter a different realm, called *talimoko*, which is said to be in the sky. Their souls are more restless and try to get in touch with the living, which is feared by the latter.

Although the religious beliefs of the Apa Tanis were clearly conceived by the upper class, the councils (*buliangs*) responsible for keeping the tribal morale high and tending to communal matters are composed of

Above and opposite, top: *Owing to the restricted area of the Apa Tani Valley the dwellings there are confined to a very limited space, which has necessitated the construction of terraced houses.*
Photograph above: G. Gessinger

members of both classes. In them decisions regarding social or ritual affairs, such as processions, feasts and communal sacrifices, are made. The most important festivals of the Apa Tanis are *morom* and *mloko*, combinations of thanksgiving and a fertility rite. They are celebrated in winter after the harvest period and in spring to commemorate the beginning of the life cycle. At *morom* many families give sumptuous feasts of merit, for which numerous mithans are sacrificed to the gods, whereupon they are divided among the villagers. Beyond its religious significance, the purpose of celebrating so lavishly—which again involves soliciting the trade of the Nishi meat suppliers—is to reduce the wealth of those who have more to a level equal to that of other families. Such feasts are also common among the Nagas and other Northeast Indian peoples (see chapter titled "Fertility through Stones and Heads"). The tradition is a means of dealing with such aspects of human nature as the exaggerated confidence and arrogance so common among the wealthy and the envy that can be felt by those who are less fortunate. Both developments must be avoided if the community spirit of such a small tribe as the Apa Tanis is to survive.

Prior to these feasts considerable pressure is put on those who are supposed to hold them. Sometimes the village council gets involved, entrusting a particular family with the task in order to sustain and strengthen communal morale. In return the host enjoys a higher social status and the prestige of being someone who has decisively contributed to the solidarity of the community, even if it has driven him to financial ruin.

As may be inferred from the agricultural activities of the Apa Tanis most events are designed to sustain and strengthen the community spirit of a particular village or even the people as a whole. Maintaining social harmony takes the highest priority in Apa Tani thought and behavior. Even Apa Tani jurisdiction was designed accordingly. It imposes different punishments for the same crime, depending on the degree to which the society at large is affected by the misdeed in question. It was common practice to punish a serf or slave who had frequently committed misdemeanors, such

Apa Tani clothes and hairstyles bear similarities to those of the Nishis, Tagins and Hill Miris. They consist of brownish-gray garments worn over short skirts, which are draped around the waist, leaving arms and legs uncovered. The hair knot on the forehead is kept in place by one or two metal needles.

Above: *Just as nose plugs are typical among Apa Tani women, the "Apa Tani tail" was common among the men of that tribe. It is an extension of the broad, red cane belt, which dangles from the man's backside. When spread out it can be used as a seat on wet ground.* Photograph: U. G. Bauer

Above: *In former times the Apa Tanis regarded their neighbors and trading partners, the Nishis, with suspicion and distrust. This attitude was not unwarranted, for the Nishis undertook many raids in Apa Tani territory because they envied their economic prosperity and the beauty of their women. This photograph, taken in the 1950s, shows a Nishi spying on Apa Tani girls working in the rice fields.*

as petty theft, and who had been perceived by many as a burden or a source of continual annoyance, by ostracizing him from society. If necessary the condemned was even sentenced to a gruesome death by being chopped into pieces and thrown into the river. Execution, however, was always preceded by less severe punishments, such as being subject to public humiliation on the *lapang*, where members of the community were allowed to spit at, scratch and even bite the accused. Recurrent offenders would have one hand and, later, even both hands cut off. Only very rarely were they banished from the Apa Tani Valley, for this would then mean criminals would remain beyond the society's control, perhaps allying themselves with the Nishis, which could have a detrimental effect on Apa Tani society.

Yet if the theft of more valuable property, such as livestock or even human beings, occurred—as an act of revenge in a conflict between two parties—the perpetuation of the quarrel was tolerated by the village council for quite some time, as long as the general peace was not disturbed and the conflict remained between the two parties. For such cases the Apa Tanis developed a unique custom called *lisudu*, which reveals astonishing parallels to the *potlatch* rituals of the Kwakiutl Indians in the northwestern United States, whereby the wealth of the Apa Tani upper class is lavishly displayed. Only through *lisudu* was a dishonored Apa Tani patrician able to

even common practice to use the possessions of one's relatives to acquire the
number of mithans necessary to win the
competition. Yet if a quarrel escalated
beyond a certain point (there have been
reports of more than 60 mithans having
been slaughtered by each party) the village
council would intervene, putting an end to
the competition in order to save both
parties from financial ruin.

In the rare instance of a quarrel between
families from different villages escalating to
the point that the villages were forced to
state their positions, a "ritual war" was
staged. For this *gambu* the opposing
villagers met in the open valley to demonstrate their superiority in the art of war.
From a great distance the opposing parties
would throw spears and shoot arrows at
each other. As soon as one warrior in each
party was seriously injured, the *gambu* was
stopped, for it was read as a sign that the
good name of the party in question had
been restored. If a wounded person died
from his injuries, the entire village felt
morally obliged to provide the family with
compensation for their loss. The Apa Tani
gambu may be compared to the European
tradition of dueling, which was a means of
settling quarrels and points of honor,
whereby strict prearranged rules were
observed by both parties.

The development of such rituals as
lisudu or *gambu*, which were ways of
dealing with conflict, is another example of
the Apa Tanis' singular ability to know what
is vitally important for the survival of their
tribe. In a small and vulnerable society an
individual's personal affairs, such as his or
her disputes with others, must not com-
promise or pose a serious threat to the society as a whole. The strategies developed by
the Apa Tanis for coping with aggression
and conflict, in which personal as well as
communal claims are taken into account,
are yet further evidence of the extraordinary
cultural achievement of this fascinating people.[2]

Apa Tanis with rain covers made from a durable fiber.
Their most distinguishing features are their tattoos
and nose plugs (yapinghules). Small wooden disks are
inserted into the outside of the nostrils of young girls.
With increasing age the disks are enlarged in dia-
meter. The woman who wears the biggest nose plugs
enjoys the most prestige. Opponents of the tradition
claim that former generations forced their female
children to undergo this torture to make them ugly,
so that the tribe would no longer be raided by the
neighboring Nishis. A small tribe such as the Apa
Tanis needed striking identification marks to preserve
its identity in a hostile environment.

vindicate his good name and reputation.
The man who opted for *lisudu* challenged
his enemy to a competition, which served to
exhibit personal wealth by its systematic and
deliberate depletion. The challenger would
open the contest by slaughtering two or
three mithans in front of his enemy's house.
The meat was left on the street for the
villagers to take. If the enemy accepted the
challenge he butchered the same number of
animals in front of the challenger's home. It
was then the challenger's task to surpass his
enemy. Thus the ritual continued. It was

THE PEOPLES OF THE SUN AND MOON

UNITED IN DONYI-POLO

*Nima lathii mason, daga yae tadavi –
Don't think that darkness overcomes
you, because the sun and the moon are
ever present . . .* (words of comfort for a
Khampa widow) [1]

Despite the many cultural differences
among the indigenous peoples of Northeast
India a number of characteristics unite
them, one of which is the belief that
animate and inanimate nature is alive and
governed by omnipresent, invisible forces.
This is reflected in the peoples' mythology
and culture, as evidenced by their philo-
sophies of life and codes of social conduct
and art, which take the form of colorful
fabric, woodcarvings and spirited dances.

According to animistic belief numerous
gods, demons and spirits inhabit the earth
and are the forces underlying its myriad
phenomena. Natural phenomena are
attributed with supernatural powers, revealing the peoples' deep-seated reverence for
wind, rain, thunder, rivers and trees. The
hierarchy of the different spirits varies from
tribe to tribe. The pantheon of many Naga
peoples of Nagaland and Manipur, for
example, includes higher deities as well,
most of whom do not inhabit the earth and

*During festivals the Angami-Nagas of Tengima don
costumes and perform dances that venerate the sun
and moon and invoke their fertility powers.*
Photograph: P. Bernard

do not exert much influence on earth's creatures. They believe that these highest
creators engendered gods who began to
populate the realms between the distant
planets and earth, and who determine the
fate of human beings. Beneath them the
sun and moon occupy special positions.
According to Konyak-Naga belief the moon
was originally very close to the earth, but
men and animals pushed it away. Oaths
taken in the name of the sun and moon are
binding, for it is believed that these celestial
bodies are vigilant witnesses of all that takes
place on earth. The rising sun is attributed
with special powers by the Chang- and Ao-
Nagas. They observe the sunrise, trace the
sun's path and determine when it will return
from its northern orbit. By incorporating an
intercalary month into their calendar the
Angami- and Chang-Nagas link the sun year
with the moon year. In contrast to other
peoples of India they consider the sun to be
female and the moon male. The rainbow is
perceived as a heavenly bridge, a means by
which the spirits can make contact with
human beings. For the Angami-Nagas it is
the path of a sky god. [2]

The thoroughly pragmatic creation myth
of the Nagas attributes human life primarily
to rare and extraordinary natural
phenomena involving the sun and moon. It
is not, however, the mere existence of the
sun and moon that is worshipped, but
rather the eclipses of these celestial bodies.
The Konyak- and other Nagas have devised
a ritual that is performed during eclipses,

whose purpose is to allay the social tensions
that may have arisen between two villages
or clans or between members of different
social classes. According to Konyak
mythology eclipses of the sun and moon are
caused by an animal, usually a frog, a tiger
or a dog, trying to devour them. One of the
villages or clans that traditionally identifies
itself with the frog, for example, encourages
the amphibian by shouting, "Eat it up! Eat
it up!" The other clan, associated with the
mighty tiger, responds by yelling, "No, don't
eat it! That is our sun!" Naturally at the end
of the eclipse the tiger clan triumphs since
the frog never manages to engulf the
sun/moon indefinitely. Thus the social order
is reestablished between the clans and the
tensions neutralized by peaceful means. [3]

Many variations of this rite exist among
the different Naga peoples, showing that
the Nagas view themselves as partaking of
cosmological events, which they observe
and interpret. However, such a ritual can be
performed only if both sides have similar
beliefs, agree to the underlying idea and
accept the participation of people from
different social classes. Evidence of the
importance of the eclipse ritual may be
found in the engravings on the poles of
Konyak *morungs*, traditional bachelors'
houses, in which frogs, tigers and sometimes hybrid creatures are shown with a
solar or lunar disc in their mouths. The
festive headdresses used by the Mao-Nagas
today recall the rising sun, while the giant
feather headgear of the Angami-Nagas

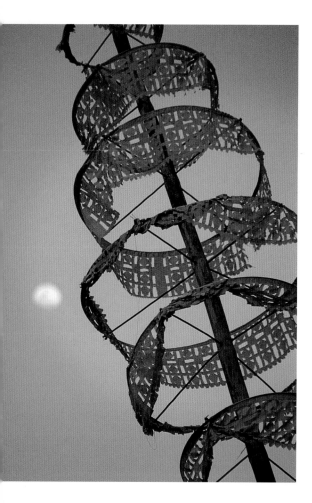

resemble the sun, with rays radiating from the center. Solar associations are also evoked by the yak felt headdresses of the Sherdukpens and the Monpas of Arunachal Pradesh, whose ends are twisted such that the rain flows from the tips, leaving the wearer relatively dry.

The Khasis of Meghalaya also attach special importance to solar eclipses. According to their tradition it is U Hinrow, the vindictive Lord of the Toads, who occasionally tries to devour Ka Sngi, the sun goddess, since she deprived him of an extra-ordinarily beautiful human child. Even today the Khasis beat drums during solar eclipses to chase away U Hinrow. One of their early myths tells of the sun and moon:

Ka Blei, the divine mistress, had four children—the sun, water, fire and moon. The moon, who once shone as brightly as the sun, was very evil. When he grew up, he began to court his sister. The sun, affronted by the spiteful behavior of her brother, took ashes from her mother's hearth and said: "Your depraved and indecent intentions are insulting! How dare you act this way against me, your elder sister, who has taken care of you for so long? Against me, Ka Sngi, who held you in her arms and carried you on her back, just like a mother? I shall smear ashes on your countenance, you wicked boy, and order you to leave the house immediately!" Ashamed and smeared with soot U Bymai, the moon, made his escape and turned pale out of sadness. Ever since the moon has emitted a pale light, and the marks to be seen on his face during full moon are the remains of the ashes that the sun smeared on his face.[4]

A famous Khasi saying alludes to this story: "Fire is female—ashes are male." Besides portraying the woman as being superior to the man, which forms the basis of the matriarchal Khasi society today, the myth reveals the strict family laws of the Khasis, which forbid liaisons between close relatives—that is, between clan members who descend from a mutual female ancestor. In Khasi society as well as in other Northeast Indian societies, incest leads to banishment, to lifelong exile from the clan and to the forfeiture of the right to be interred in the clan grave. In the early 20th century, Catholic missionaries tried to break this taboo by allowing baptized members of the same clan to intermarry, which tradition-bound clans adamantly rejected, causing

many Christianized Khasis to revert to their original religions.[5]

Great religious importance is attached to the sun and moon in the other states of Northeast India as well. In a story that traces the etymology of the state name of "Tripura" the name is purported to derive from that of the sun god Tripuradhana.[6] Moreover, the chronicles of the Tripuri kings reveal evidence of star worship. They tell of the first emperors of the Tripuras, who were the descendants of Druhya, the third son of Yayati of the moon dynasty.[7] Only the Reangs, the second largest tribe in Tripura, are entitled to perform a special ritual in the most important Tripureshwari temple in Udaipur. At every new moon they gather in small groups at the temple to light bamboo fires, which are intended to summon the moon to reappear.[8] For the Tripuris, Tripura's largest indigenous tribe, the *surya darshan*, or "sun ritual," marks the end of the postnatal taboo period. Women of the Morasings wear a silver half-moon-shaped ring in their noses to distinguish themselves from the women of other tribes. The Sutradhars from western Tripura trace their roots to "Karna, the son of Kunti, who descended from the sun goddess before she married Pandu."[9]

Assam looks back on a long tradition of the sun cult. The Brahmaputra Valley, which was inhabited by Hindus very early on, is referred to as the "land of the sunrise" in the great Indian epics (ca. 600–500 B.C.). The temples there are described as important places of pilgrimage. Yet not only Assam, formerly called Pragyotisha, the land where the sun first touches Indian soil every morning, is mentioned, but also the sun as the highest god. Mount Shri Surya is located in Goalpara in western Assam, which in the *Puranas* is described as the "eternal homeland of the sun." Indeed many temples in Assam, the majority of which are now mere ruins, were consecrated to the sun. The largest one is located in Tezpur in central Assam. Its main image has been identified as the "sun god," dating from the first century A.D., when Buddhism began to spread in Assam. Dhitika, the first Buddhist missionary in Assam, succeeded in converting the people to the new faith by telling them that he too was a follower of the sun cult. Moreover when Vaishnavism started taking hold in Assam (sixth century A.D.) its highest god was associated with the sun and fire but later was deprived of this symbolism.[10] Traces of the ancient sun

Top: *A shattra, a bamboo totem erected by the Meitheis to commemorate the* Umanglais, *the sylvan deities, or a deceased relative.* Bottom: *In Meghalaya the half-moon-shaped sword is regarded as the symbol of female power.* Photograph: T. Ernsting, Bilderberg.

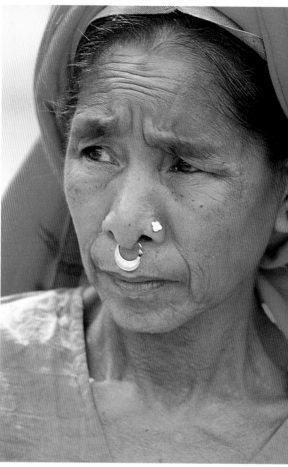

and fire cults are to be found in the harvest rituals of some of the peoples of Assam as well as in dances performed during the national holiday of Bihu.

Despite the fact that the Meitheis, Manipur's dominant population, are Hindus, they worship Sanamahi, a variation of the ancient sun goddess of such mountain peoples as the Kabui-, the Mao- and the Thangkul-Nagas, who venerate her together with the god of fire. The Meithei performances of the *rasa-lila* dramas include explicit references to the sunset, the full moon and sunrise, and the main entrance of all the state's temples are positioned such that they face the rising sun.[11]

In Arunachal Pradesh the Tangsas of the Tirap District recount that in the beginning neither day nor night existed, for the sun and moon gods took turns illuminating the sky. Moreover, according to Padam-Adi legend, the moon appeared on the eastern horizon as soon as the sun set in the west. For them the mighty Brahmaputra River is the sister of the sun.[12] The Akas have a rich heritage of myths involving the sun and moon. Their ancestor, Awa, is said to have been entirely covered with thick

A yet to be fully excavated sandstone sculpture depicting Surya, the sun god, with the solar disc to the right of his head (late Gupta style ca. eighth century A.D., Pilak region, west Tripura).

fur, which made him very ugly. By means of cunning, however, he succeeded in marrying the sun's ravishing daughter in order to provide human beings with all hey would need to live. The Akas even associate the sun and moon with death, as revealed in one of their lyrical and enchanting myths:

> Once there were two suns and two moons in the sky, one each being female and one each being male. The sun's wife and the moon's husband fell in love with each other and, since they could not meet in the sky, they used to come down to

Top right: *Morasing women from Tripura adorn themselves with half-moon nose rings.*
Bottom: *Tulasibong—an altar for the sun god, erected in the courtyard of a Meithei home near Lake Loktak.*

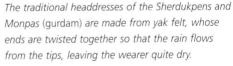

The traditional headdresses of the Sherdukpens and Monpas (gurdam) are made from yak felt, whose ends are twisted together so that the rain flows from the tips, leaving the wearer quite dry.

Above and opposite: The festive costumes of the Akas bear witness to their belief in the sun and moon as the highest gods. The central disc of the headgear (lenchhi) recalls the sun, while the chains resemble the sun's rays. The horn-shaped jewelry adorning their ears (rombins) symbolizes the moon while the earrings (gichli) represent the lunar orbit.

earth. When they met there, everything around them caught fire, and that is why there is red and yellow soil. Two mighty brothers decided to bring the treacherous rendezvous to an end and shot arrows at the two luminous lovers. The sun's wife was struck dead on the spot, but the moon's husband, though seriously wounded, managed to escape into the skies, where he died in the arms of his wife, who wept bitterly. The sun saw all this misery and warned the beings on earth not to answer the tears of the

moon's wife once she appeared in the firmament that night, otherwise death would also strike the creatures of the earth forever. When darkness descended the moon's wife ascended with her deceased husband in her arms. All human beings and animals were asleep, except for the barking deer and the peacock. Moved by the moon's wife's bitter tears they asked her what was ailing her. Hearing this, the moon's wife let go of her husband and shouted: "Thus as you have killed my husband, thus all of you,

humans, animals and birds, shall not escape death!" When the cock heard what had happened to the world that night, he roused the sun, calling to him to help. The sun came out of his house and saw that men and animals were weeping. But there was nothing he could do, since the barking deer and peacock had not heeded his command. To the present day cocks call at the sun every morning to ask him to lift the curse of death from the creatures of the earth.[13]

Over the centuries the peoples of the central belt of Arunachal Pradesh, comprising the Subansiri, Siang and Dibang Valley Districts, did not have much contact with each other—and, when they did, it was usually when at war with each other. Thus, they have remained culturally distinct and independent of each other. Curiously, however, they are united in the belief that the sun and moon are the highest deities. Among the 30 different Adi groups, the Mishmis, the Tagins, the Nishis, the Hill Miris and the Apa Tanis, this concept has evolved into a unique religion—Donyi-Poloism.

Little is known about this animistic-shamanistic religion. It is probably the unwitting achievement of the Christian missionaries, who, in the days of British colonial rule, tried to convert the mountain peoples to Christianity, often employing deceitful means. This resulted in the state government issuing a decree forbidding all missionary activities in the region. Intellectuals began to revert to their original values and to do everything in their power to preserve and perpetuate Donyi-Poloism. The

Adis are credited with this development, for they are in the process of recording and summarizing the various myths and traditions of the region that have been passed down orally by shamans (*nyibus*) in epic hymns since time immemorial. The aim is to publish them in written form and to make the people, particularly the younger generation, more aware of their cultural heritage and to supplement this knowledge with that of other religions and concepts.

To its followers Donyi-Poloism is not a man-made religion, for it has neither prophets nor a human founder. The highest god of the religion, Donyi-Polo (sun-moon), is believed to have founded the religion himself, which is thought to have existed since the beginning of the world. Donyi-Polo, considered to be the center of love, assumes the forms of the celestial bodies of the sun and moon. The fact that all aspects of life—good, evil, heaven and hell—exist beneath *donyi* (sun) and *polo* (moon) makes Donyi-Polo omnipotent, omnipresent and omniscient.

In the beginning, according to the followers of Donyi-Poloism, Donyi-Polo existed in the form of a luminary body and nothingness and silence prevailed. The desire to create a universe caused the luminary body to break in two. One part became the firmament, revered as the father, the other became Mother Earth. Donyi-Polo remained between the sky and the earth as Creator, Protector and Destroyer. It is said that, by connecting heaven and earth through his mere existence, which is tantamount to the notion of union, all living beings and inanimate objects were created, as well as the father of humankind, Abotani. With him Taki, the leader of evil spirits, Taro, Abotani's brother, as well as lions, tigers and elephants issued from the womb of Mother Earth.

After the creation of the universe, the Almighty Donyi-Polo ascended into the sky in the form of five suns. The searing heat destroyed everything on earth: the rivers dried up, the grass and trees were burnt. Through this demise and destruction every creature experienced the Almighty powers

of Donyi-Polo. Except for Abotani all beings beseeched the head of the demons to slay Donyi-Polo, but Donyi-Polo's omniscience prevented this. A second effort, made by another challenger, named Tame, likewise failed. As punishment Donyi-Polo entered Tame's stomach. Tame could not bear the burning sensation the Almighty caused inside him, so he prayed for forgiveness and accepted the supremacy of Donyi-Polo, who proceeded to take leave of Tame's body through his anus to return to His own kingdom. Immediately thereafter darkness fell over the entire universe. Again it became increasingly difficult for creatures on the earth to survive. In realizing the supremacy of Donyi-Polo they began to worship him. (Another version of this myth tells of a great flood that was accompanied by cold, hunger and illness, which could be staved off only by worshipping Donyi-Polo.)

Upon hearing from the heavenly messengers of the insufferable life of all the creatures on earth, the Almighty Donyi-Polo decided to allow only a single sun to rise each day and only one moon at night but issued a warning to all not to come out on the first day of the sun's rising. Yet not a single creature on earth, not even Abotani, could resist the temptation. Irate about the creatures' disobedience, Donyi-Polo spoke: "O man! Thy have violated my commandments. Thus thy shall suffer from every cause from this day onward. Thy shall experience the life of blindness, lameness, dumbness, sorrow and pain, and shall meet unseen diseases, and death is certain!"

In order to propagate the human races Abotani underwent various marital tests, none of which proved to be of use, for he did not have the blessing of Donyi-Polo. Finally he decided to marry Donyi-Yai, Donyi-Polo's first, and beautiful, daughter. Since Abotani was by nature very clever, intelligent and shrewd he managed to win Donyi-Yai's hand by means of cunning. With Donyi-Polo's blessings the human couple, who had a direct link to the Almighty, were able to multiply into many races and to spread across the earth. Thus all human races descend from Abotani and, therefore, have a direct link to Donyi-Polo.

When praying to Donyi-Polo it is not deemed necessary to fold one's hands or to kneel down. Followers of Donyi-Poloism believe that direct communication can be established with the Almighty anytime, anywhere. Rituals are required only to appease the numerous lesser deities and

Although the Naga peoples do not consider the sun and moon to be the highest gods, their costumes reveal the most striking solar and lunar symbolism. Left: Mao-Nagas performing the cosmic dance and wearing headdresses resembling the rays of the rising sun. Photographs: P. Nalin. Above: A Thangkul-Naga chief in his luhupa headgear, decorated with red crab's-eye seeds. In addition a brass disc, Job's-tears seeds, white-glass seed beads, black human hair fringe and hornbill tail feathers are fixed to a cane-and-cloth frame that recalls a half moon, the sun and the planets. Photograph: P. Bernard

Angami-Nagas from the village of Tengima in their lavish costumes. The headdresses resembling the sun are so heavy that they must be held in front of the face by ropes. Photographs: V. J. Patel (left) and P. Bernard (right).

spirits, most of which are evil in character and hostile toward man. Furthermore it is believed that anyone who prays to Donyi-Polo will be blessed, for nothing is possible without His blessing. Donyi-Poloism has a practical moral code, which boils down to four basic tenets:

Menyi Menma Beka—Speak no evil,
Tanyi Tama Beka—Hear no evil,
Kanyi Kama Beka—See no evil,
Rinyi Rima Beka—Do no evil.

Heeding these commandments is thought to lead to self-realization, to a life devoid of fear and to one's admittance into heaven (*Donyi-Polo Moko*); violating them ends in being banished to hell (*Uyu-mora*). From these basic commandments ethical precepts have been distilled to which the followers of Donyi-Poloism are encouraged to aspire, such as equality, liberty, justice and knowledge. They believe in feeling one with the universe, universal brotherhood and love for all. In the eyes of every Donyi-Polian all beings are the children of the Almighty Donyi-Polo; no one is regarded as either superior or inferior to others, for all are equal in the eyes of the Almighty Donyi-Polo.[14]

5

The House — The Womb

Which other being opposing the ubiquitous law of gravity should catch the childlike attention more than the flame kindled by himself?
It is the fireplace where man feels externally as safe as internally within his good conscience and thoughts.
(H. Kuekelhaus)[1]

This passage alludes to the profoundly mysterious element that unites nearly all the peoples of Northeast India and continues to be of vital importance to them to this day: fire. From time immemorial man has been magically attracted to fire. It invariably draws his gaze into its flames. Indeed most people, when sitting around a fire for some time, begin to brood or let their thoughts wander. The flickering flames and incandescent glow of this elusive element induce a curious state of calm and reflection in its beholders, in which the laws of space and time do not seem to obtain. This state of mind is brought about because we innately associate the fireplace with security and shelter: fire keeps out the night and its menacing shadows, dark chill, wild animals and hostile neighbors. The people who gather around it are dear to us, our closest relatives, friends and acquaintances—all those who do not pose a threat to us. The fireplace is a place of comfort, security and

A Nocte from Kheti joining the festivities around the fireplace in the chief's house.

familiarity. The side averted from the fire, however, remains vulnerable. The dangers of the night begin immediately beyond the fire's glow. This is probably why prehistoric man took to inhabiting caves. A fire lit at the cave's entrance protected those who were gathered around it from the animals of the night, for the cave was safe, as a pre-liminary exploration of it would certainly have established. The limited number of caves might have provided the impetus for man to build the first rudimentary shelters. The essential, primal and almost cavelike character of the first dwellings made by man can also be discerned in the dark long-houses of Northeast India. Besides sheltering its inhabitants from external dangers, a house, with all its warmth and coziness, restores the sense of security once felt inside the mother's womb—it is a more sophisticated form of the cave, which served to diminish man's feelings of insecurity and fear that resulted from being expelled from the womb. Indeed fire— which, on account of its color and the heat it produces, is comparable to the sun—and the tubular longhouse architecture of North-east India is symbolic of the widely held belief in a female god, known as the "Great Mother" (see chapter titled "Women's Mysterious Realm"). But only the sacred, unbreakable laws of hospitality, which were developed in connection with the fireplace, and which secured man's continuance, have led to the symbolic meaning of the fireplace as it has been pointed out in this chapter's

introductory quotation–the fireplace as the external symbol of man's internal good conscience and thoughts.

Around this central, communal point— the fireplace, or the hearth—a fascinating and sophisticated longhouse culture has developed among many of the Northeast Indian peoples, such as the Nishis, the Hill Miris, the Akas, the Mishmis, the Noctes, the Wanchos, the various Adi peoples of Arunachal Pradesh, the Naga peoples of Nagaland and Manipur, the Garos of Meghalaya and, in former times, the tribes inhabiting the territory now known as Mizo-ram. This type of society is also encountered in southern China, Vietnam, Laos, Cambodia, Thailand, Burma and Indonesia, and is even found among some of the jungle dwellers of South America. The reasons for its development are manifold.

In general it may be said that the longhouse serves the communal spirit of a particular group, first and foremost the fam-ily. In Hill Miri society, for example, it was not uncommon for one householder to live with up to 15 wives and 40 children in a single longhouse. In recent years this form of cohabitation has become rare, so that now only three women per man, along with their children, live together. For the later wives the man has separate houses built, where he takes turns visiting them.

The families of independent, bellicose and proud peoples, such as the Nishis in the Subansiri District or the Mishmis in the Lohit and Dibang Valley Districts of Arunachal

Pradesh, also live together in up to 90-m-long houses. Their definition of family, however, is broader and includes all relatives of the same family line. Accordingly up to 20 related families—a clan—such as those of several brothers or cousins, together with their servants and, in earlier times, their slaves, reaching up to 100 people in total, may inhabit a Nishi longhouse. A Nishi family consists of one man, several wives and their unmarried children. The extended family inhabits separate parts of the house. They are independent of the family of the

householder and not subordinate to him, although the householder is held in high esteem.

Furthermore every family is financially autonomous in that it owns separate areas of the forest for hunting or fields for cultivating. However this does not mean that economic or family ties do not matter to these families or do not hold them together. In accordance with unwritten tribal laws families living together under a single roof are obliged to help each other in the fields when necessary. They also help

The first fireplace seen when entering a house is the most prestigious one in many tribal households (Apa Tani).

Opposite, top: A Tutsa boy next to the morung wall, where such important ritual items as shoulder blades and jaw bones are stored. Opposite, bottom: Konyak village council of Mon in session, over which chief (Ang) Yangbong presides.

each other hunt and fish and attend ritual functions together. Communal institutions, such as village elders or councils, are unknown to the Nishis. Unlike other tribal societies in Northeast India, who regard themselves as a single social unit, it is not uncommon in Nishi society for a fight to arise between households, which, in former times, often ended in considerable bloodshed. Moreover, owing to the many inhabitants of a longhouse, not many houses are needed in a longhouse "village"—sometimes they comprise no more than one or two.[2]

For the Adis communal solidarity means something else. In addition to the longhouses, which are the focal point of the family, certain houses are designated the domiciles of the youth, from the age of ten to the marrying age. In these boys' *moshups* and girls' *rashengs* children learn from their elder housemates what is expected of them and how they are to behave in society. These community houses are the social center of every village. In them people from different age groups form natural working teams. The rights and duties of every member are determined by his or her age. Girls and boys are not strictly segregated. On

the contrary, the young men often visit the girls in their *rashengs*, where the first romantic ties are formed.[3] As in Naga society, which have similar institutions, called *morungs*, the longhouse culture is based on pedagogical precepts. Another reason for its establishment might have been to prevent incestuous attachments from forming, which, in the long run, could pose serious threats to the survival of a clan. Consequently incest is one of the most deeply ingrained social taboos in Adi as well as Naga society. Interestingly enough, however, until very recently, married life among certain Adi groups was marked by polyandry, whereby a woman took several brothers as husbands.

The community houses also function as social institutions, where, for example, the old and infirm residents of the village may live and be treated. Inside or in front of them the biggest festivals are held. In some Naga groups the heads taken during raids used to be stored there. In many Nocte and Wancho villages they still house the up to 20-m-long log drums, which are closely linked with the head-hunting tradition (see chapter titled "Fertility… ") and are played by the village's male population during festivals and ritual ceremonies. Nowadays trophies, such as animal skulls or the highly prized shoulder blades of mithan buffaloes, are still stored there.

The longhouse is where the traditional village councils (*kebangs* in Adi) convene. Even today they manage all administrative and legal affairs of the village. They are largely informal institutions to which all persons of a certain social standing automatically belong. Originally probably a shamanistic institution, the *kebangs* lost any religious significance they might have had centuries ago.[4]

In Mizoram the social aspect of the former youth dormitories (*zawlbuks*) has clearly survived. Although the members of so-called youth clubs do not live in the large, modern houses, they do meet there regularly to discuss and make decisions on certain matters. As Mizoram's native inhabitants were christianized, their traditional culture and religion were neglected, almost to the point of having been irrevocably lost to posterity. Today they feel just as responsible for reviving these traditions as they do for organizing the tribe's social activities, which can be traced back to the Christian notion of charity.

In Northeast Indian tribal societies other types of longhouse also existed, some of which served to accommodate the village chief and his family. Social rank and wealth, as well as the idea of being able to give shelter to strangers and to people in need, were factors that led to the erection of houses reaching 40 m in length. In this context mention must be made of the last extant large house in Meghalaya's Khasi society. It is inhabited by the high priestess of the Smit village. In it she walks around in complete darkness, executes the ritual duties necessary for the benefit of the entire village and is constantly in contact with the

Above: *In many tribal societies the main poles of community houses, such as* moshups *or* morungs, *are adorned with objects that symbolize fertility. Shown here is a buffalo skull and horns, hanging in a community house in the Minyong-Adi village of Yeksi.*

Top left: *The Wancho chief's abode in Nginu is some 60 m long. The naturally perforated roof and walls let light into the house.*

Top right: *Among the Tutsas great importance is attached to lighting festival fires in the traditional manner, without the aid of matches or lighters.*

Top: *The interior of a morung in the Wancho village of Wakka. The symbolically important main poles of the house bear carvings depicting two warriors and their totems, tigers. A bas-relief of a tiger biting a snake adorns the main cross beam above which firewood is stored. The entrance leads directly to the large log-drum; near the side entrance a large collection of buffalo skulls can be seen.* Photograph: G. Horter. Bottom: *The interior of a Zemi-Naga morung.* Photograph: P. Bernard.

Right, from top to bottom: *The last traditional Khasi house, located in the village of Smit, is the residence of the Khasi high priestess. A Wancho morung in the village of Pongchau. The stone piles in front of the hut represent the female power of fertility. The wooden beams leaning against the walls symbolize the male principle. A lavishly carved morung in Mokokchung, Nagaland, bearing depictions of tigers, human beings, hornbills and buffalo skulls.* Photograph: P. Nalin. *The chief's house in Maram Khullen, Manipur, ornately adorned with buffalo skulls and carvings.*

spirits and ancestors.

How the first house was constructed is told in a beautiful myth of the Singphos:

In the days when men lived in caves and under trees, two friends, Kindru-Lalim and Kincha Lali-Dam, decided to build a house for themselves. Unfortunately they had no idea how to go about it, so they went to the forest to consult the animals. The first animal they met was Elephant, who spoke unto them: "Cut wooden pillars as strong and thick as my legs!"

Snake told them: "Cut poles as long and thin as myself!" The friends went on and met a mithan, mourning over the carcass of her dead husband, who had been killed by Tiger. Her answer to the friends' question was: "Make cross-poles and a roof like the bones of this skeleton!" By Fish they were told: "Look at the scales on my back. Get plenty of leaves and put them on the roof, one on top of the other like my scales!" When the two friends heard all this they knew how they would build their first house. . .[5]

The morning mist rising from the rainforests below this typical Hill Miri village, built on a mountain slope east of the town of Raga.
Photograph: A. Dilwali

Opposite, from top to bottom: *Several house types in Arunachal Pradesh: The houses of the Apa Tanis have wooden roofs, as in this village, Hari.* Photograph: H. Sanghvi. *A Hill Miri longhouse near Raga.* Photograph: G. Gessinger. *A solitary Nishi longhouse. Sherdukpen houses in Dirang Dzong.*

framework of vertical and horizontal poles forms the walls of the longhouse. Bamboo bands are interwoven through the framework, resembling the construction of the floors.

The high rains naturally require that the roofs are constructed at an angle. The materials used to build the roofs vary from people to people, according to what is available to them. In many regions whole or half bamboo poles are laid next to each other and tied together. Well designed bamboo constructions are partly or entirely sealed with tar, covered with several layers of straw and braced against the wind with horizontal beams. In lower regions, where villages are not nearly as affected by the wind and other elements, simple bamboo mats sometimes suffice. Remarkably all the traditional houses—be they a simple granary or a 90-m-long longhouse—can be built without using a single nail. The design and length of Northeast Indian longhouses bear a striking resemblance to those of the people of Borneo. In contrast to the houses of Borneo and Malaysia, however, the traditional grass roofs and bamboo-paneled walls still are the rule rather than the exception among the Nishis and other peoples of Arunachal Pradesh. The use of durable though ugly corrugated iron roofs has not caught on, at least not yet.

The interior of a longhouse measures 3 m to 4 m in height, from floor to ceiling. Most of this space, especially above the fireplaces, is used to store provisions in swinging racks that hang from the ceiling and are also used for drying firewood. The number of fireplaces indicates either the number of families living together in one house or the number of wives the householder has. The first fireplace seen upon entering the interior via the extended verandah is the most important and prestigious one. It is considered sacred and is tended by the wife of the house-builder, that is, the first wife of the polygamous householder. Apart from the light that streams through the cracks of the bamboo mat, the fireplaces are the only sources of light in the usually pitch-dark rooms, for, with the exception of the entranceway, openings, such as windows, are rare. Chimneys do not exist. The rising smoke covers the entire interior with a layer of black soot, which contributes to the dim atmosphere of the dwelling and to the relatively low life expectancy of the people.

The reason for this lack of windows and

Owing to the mountainous terrain and the flooding during the monsoon months a traditional Northeast Indian longhouse is by and large a pile dwelling. Man-high piles support a hardwood frame with the necessary number of transversal girders that run the length of the house. A structure of braided bamboo bands rests on this, and is fitted to the girders with bamboo belts. Through this elastic bamboo "mattress" light and fresh air are able to enter the room. As a surface on which to sleep the floor is comparable to a hard mattress. A

Top: *Pile dwellings such as this Reang tong are common in Tripura owing to the heavy rains brought by the monsoons.*
Center: *The floor of a Molsum-Halam house.*
Bottom: *Like most Northeast Indian longhouses this Mogh house has been built without a single nail.*

In most tribal communities the construction of a new house is undertaken by the entire male population of the village and usually does not take longer than a few days. Top: *The foundations of this house in the Nocte village of Laho has been laid, its bamboo floor constructed and its pillars erected. The bamboo cross beams are secured to two pillars, which will bear the weight of the central roof beams.*
Bottom: *The same house one day later. The roof will be covered with dried leaves of the toko tree, a fan-like palm tree that grows in abundance near the village.* Photographs: G. Horter.

chimneys is the prevailing opinion that, wherever light finds its way in, so do wind and cold. Darkness and warmth are deemed eminently more preferable. In view of the fact that the average rainy season in the Indian rainforests lasts for six months, it is understandable that the native architects do everything in their power to waterproof their grass-covered houses and have refrained from incorporating windows and chimneys into the buildings. Moreover it is also understandable that the tribes that, until recently, were not familiar with metal processing, except through imported jewelry and the production of simple blades, have not been able to design metal chimneys or smoke outlets as yet.

A further reason for longhouses having only one opening, the door, is that it prevents thieves entering the house. If the houses had more entrances the people living inside them would be even more afraid of having their belongings stolen than they are already. In some societies this fear has led to the habit of keeping only a few personal belongings inside the house. The Hill Miris are known for burying their possessions in secret locations in the jungle. Besides burglary, frequent fires caused by inadequate ventilation are perhaps another reason why some clans prefer to store their belongings in the jungle. If a house burns down the spirit responsible for the incident must first be appeased by the shaman. During this ritual the family finds shelter in a neighbor's house. Only after the observance of a certain taboo period may reconstruction begin, which is always undertaken by the entire village or clan.

Besides kitchen utensils the only furnishings to be found in a traditional longhouse are bamboo and cane baskets, which vary in size and shape and are used to store clothes or blankets. The walls are used to display cult objects, which, in former times, included enemies' skulls. Today cultic animal trophies are stored there, such as buffalo or monkey heads, mithan horns and shoulder blades, deer antlers, boar jaws, monkey hands and tails, tiger, leopard and goat furs and elephant tusks. They are the pride of the family and are used in bartering.

One might think that, aside from the security that living in a longhouse has to offer, life shared with so many people in a relatively small area could be rather problematic when it comes to personal freedom, sexuality and disagreements between clan members, such as mothers-in-law or rival brothers. Certainly such communal life is full of conflict. Yet, as in other rural societies, which, until relatively recently, also dominated the Western world, community spirit is held in higher esteem than self-realization or individualism. Communal life is not considered to be oppressive. On the contrary, the people of Northeast India equate being alone with being lonely. The fact that there is always someone to talk to makes the confined living conditions and restricted privacy worthwhile. Longhouse society is a way of communal life that has developed

The home of a Mao-Naga who has given an entire series of feasts of merit, which entitles him to adorn the facade of his house with cross beams and these naive yet expressive carvings, which depict the ancient symbols of fertility: mithan buffalo heads and horns and human heads.

over the ages out of economic necessity.

Certain traditions concerning these economic necessities have also evolved over time and bear witness to the community spirit that is deemed more important than, for example, personal wealth. In many societies, land is transferred to the owner's successor quite early on, enabling the latter to see to the financial affairs of the clan in his best years. Ethical matters, however, remain the responsibility of the eldest of the clan. Owing to his long life experience he is believed to make the wisest and best decisions—an ability for which he is held in high esteem.

Some clans are aware of the difficulties that can arise between spouses and in-laws, and have devised means of separating them for a certain period. The participation of women until old age in the economic vitality

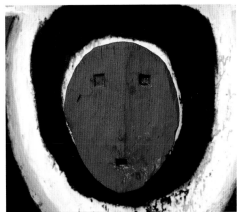

of the tribe—found, for example, among the Meghalayan Khasis and Manipuri Meitheis, the latter of whom conceived the idea of the Ima market in Imphal (see chapter titled "Women's Mysterious Realm")—has certainly served to relieve tensions between spouses and mothers-in-law.

In most tribal societies premarital sex is taboo—nevertheless, it is not uncommon. Divorce among most Northeast Indian peoples is a very humane affair and never leads to the social ostracism or financial ruin of either party. Inside the house the resi-

dents—perhaps out of necessity—regard sex as a matter of course. Members of longhouse communities are of course aware of the sexual activities of their housemates, an inevitable result of the confined living quarters. The desire to be sheltered from the outside world, be it from the elements or hostile neighbors, always was and had to be stronger than the sense of shame resulting from a lack of privacy. In the rarer polyandrous families, in which between two and five brothers share the same wife, this delicate situation is dealt with such that the women are in charge and the men must heed their commands. The hard physical labor required of the members of rural societies, coupled with the large quantities of alcohol that are consumed by many indigenous peoples, do the rest to neutralize the situation.

One might assume that social problems arise on account of the fact that the bamboo houses fail to keep neighbors from hearing what goes on inside them. However, since the villagers are not informed merely about the sexual activities of their neighbors, but also their ailments, deaths, births and marriages—in short, the

good and bad times of everyone—and the sense of village solidarity is strong, there is no reason to feel ashamed or embarrassed.

Such unabashed naturalness is also reflected in the custom of men and women wearing no more than mere loincloths as clothes, which is common among many tribes in Tripura, Nagaland and southern Arunachal Pradesh. In a Nocte village in Arunachal Pradesh's Tirap District adolescents are even prohibited from wearing clothes until they have reached a certain age. Only since contact has been established with the "outside world" have such tribes as the Apa Tanis begun to question their traditional forms of communal living. These are the first warning signs of the decline of a traditional life-style—a social system that has evolved over time and has enabled the indigenous peoples to lead contented and uncomplicated lives, far removed indeed from feelings of self-consciousness, guilt or shame.

Two Konyak-Naga girls on their way to the fields of Changlangsho. Photograph: P. Nalin

The traditional Wancho village of Wakka is situated on a hilltop in the extreme south of the Tirap District of Arunachal Pradesh. This strategic location enabled the villagers to keep vigilant watch over the valleys below—a necessary precautionary measure on account of the head-hunting tradition in the area. Photograph: G. Horter.

Top right: *An old photograph of a Garo* borang—*a watchtower built in a tree.* Top left and above: *Two Garo longhouses in Chidaogre, West Garo hills, Meghalaya.* Kimas *posted in front of the house remind visitors of its deceased owner.*

Top left: *An Idu-Mishmi longhouse at Aohali,*
Dibang Valley District, Arunachal Pradesh. Below:
The Wancho chief's house at Nginu, Tirap District,
Arunachal Pradesh. In the foreground is the former
"head tree," where, after raids, captured heads
were put on display like trophies.

Upper right: *As was once common among many*
Naga peoples, the Noctes of Laju village still shape
the thatching straw around the main poles of the
morungs into human figures—thus emphasizing the
purpose of the morungs, which is where a person
becomes human.

6

IN HEAVEN AS ON EARTH

THE MYTHOLOGY OF WEAVING

I do not agree with the criticism that the preservation of tribal art and tribal dress indicates a desire to keep the tribal people as museum specimens. The danger is that these people will lose their culture and have nothing to replace it. (J. Nehru)[1]

Northeast India is not noted for its architecture. Magnificent temples, for which the rest of India is so well known, are not to be found here. Instead the culture of this region reveals itself in small things, most notably its folklore, which, in turn, is reflected in the peoples' dances and textiles. Indeed a remarkable number of stories told in this region serve to explain the genesis of weaving. Several of them are recounted here:

In the beginning only Donyi-Polo, the sun-moon god, knew about the art of weaving. He taught it to a female spirit, who, flattered by the opulent sacrifices offered to her by Abotani, the first man, went to his wife in a dream and showed her how to weave.
(Bori-Adi)

In the beginning human beings were covered with hair. In the course of time they stripped it off, using it to weave cloth. Later, when all the hair had been

Mizos in festive dress.

used up, they resorted to a nettle, from which they made yarn.
(Taraon-Mishmi)

The Spider was the first weaver in the world. It was by watching it spin its web that the women became proficient in the art and the men learned to span rivers with cane suspension bridges.
(Singpho)

The first weaver was a girl named Hambrumai, who was taught the art by the god Matai. She took her designs from the waves and ripples of water, from the patterns created by tree branches, bamboo leaves, ferns and flowers. One day, however, Hairum, the Porcupine, saw her cloth and came to steal it from her cave. The entrance was too narrow for him, so he pushed the rock into the river, crushing the girl beneath it. Her loom was broken into pieces and carried by the current downstream to the plains, where the people there found them and learned to weave. But the designs of Hambrumai were not rent asunder. They turned into butterflies, and today you can still see the patterns she once made, in the markings on their wings.
(Kaman-Mishmi)

For the people of Northeast India textiles and jewelry are not merely matters of fashion or decoration. A woven garment, a

carved wooden amulet, a bracelet, a necklace or a belt are status symbols and indicate to which tribe the wearer belongs; yet they also take up mythological motifs as well as those specific to the artist's environment, some of which are rendered in abstract shapes. The most figurative images are those found in the woven and embroidered cloth of the Wanchos, the Khamptis, the Monpas and the Sherdukpens of Arunachal Pradesh as well as the Nagas of Nagaland and Manipur.

In the fabric designs of the Tibetan-Buddhist peoples the most common motifs are animals, such as crocodiles, tortoises, frogs, fish, birds and elephants, and human beings, or combinations of both, such as a person on horseback. Abstract elements, such as zigzags, rhombs, triangles and squares, which form the basic patterns of Northeast Indian fabric, are replete with symbolism, even if this has played a less important role in recent years.

The motifs bear witness to the artists' extraordinary capacity for abstraction. They reveal the worldview of the artists who conceived them, for whom an abstract form, a symbol, represents a path leading to a higher truth. The symbolism of Northeast Indian tribes reveals remarkable parallels to that of other "primitive" peoples. The powers of expression inherent in such symbolism was rediscovered in the early 20th century by Western abstract artists, for whom it served as a fountainhead of creative inspiration.

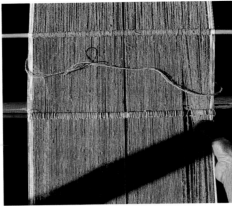

This food is the corona, represented by lines projecting from the central body of the design. The sun is transformed into a flower in the *jana* motif of the Akas:

Once a Tibetan Raja was so great that he was able to talk to the sun. He had a palace, open on all four sides, which was so large that it could accommodate the sun. Every day he was born at the rising of the sun; by midday he grew into a youth; by evening he was old and descended into the darkness with the sun. The next morning he was born again. When he finally left the earth, the multicolored jana *flower sprang up in his palace.*

The Naga peoples adorn their textiles with cowry shells, which represent the moon and the heads of slain enemies. The source of this symbolism is the fertility cult, which is an integral part of Naga culture. The tradition of head-hunting was thought to preserve and revive fertility in the people and fecundity in the fields. Since the cultivation of crops and human conception are influenced by the cyclical phases of the moon, it seems only logical to associate the moon with the human head, which, according to Naga belief, is the source of fertility. This symbolic equation shows that the indigenous peoples believe worldly events are inextricably linked with cosmic forces, with which they wish to live in harmony. Woven patterns are thought to express the knowledge and understanding of such correspondences.

All things cosmic are believed to have earthly equivalents. A row of striped squares on the cloth of the Mishmis in eastern Arunachal Pradesh, for example, represents the sky and stars; at the same time it also symbolizes a slithering snake that has left its mark on the soil. Therefore the snake is believed to live in harmony with the cosmic plan—a revelation of the Mishmi woman weaver to which the cloth attests. Correspondences are likewise thought to exist between various earthly phenomena and are also depicted on woven articles. A triangle might stand for a mountain or bam-

Many textile designs reflect the social and religious systems of the tribe from which they originate. Accordingly the stringent and straight lines in Apa Tani and Adi fabric attest to the confined living quarters of these tribes and stand in clear contrast to the diverse patterns of the highly individualized Mishmis. Other designs can be understood as an artist's attempt to depict, and therefore re-create, the world around him. For this reason numerous motifs are drawn from everyday life and depict natural phenomena and such quotidian objects as ropes, coal tongs, flowers, shrubs and bamboo leaves. This does not mean, however, that these images are devoid of symbolic meaning. Many of the weaving designs of the Monpas and the Sherdukpens reveal aspects of their Tibetan-Buddhist life-styles. Temples, prayer flags, yak heads and the "Chinese fence," a border design thought to protect them from their mighty neighbor, China, are discernible in their textiles.

Motifs depicted on ritual garments are of a purely symbolic nature. The spiral, for example, a shape that stands for the link between earth and the divine realm, is frequently embroidered on shamans' capes. The designs on garments worn by Lamaist monks during masked dances likewise have exclusively symbolic functions. The fabric of the "simple people," however, also depicts such a path to the celestial world: for the Monpas and the Sherdukpens *swastikas* are the ancient symbol of the sun and, at the same time, the wheel of life in Indian and Tibetan cosmology. Notable also are the symbols of the sun and moon encountered in Aka and Naga textiles, in which a nine-sided rhomb represents the sun with a corona. This motif can be traced to the following myth:

Above: *A Tangkhul woman at her loom, beginning what will eventually become an exquisite garment.*
Photographs: P. Nalin
Opposite, from top left to right center: *The traditional silk weaving of Assam and Tripura requires elaborate looms. Since fine and raw silk has only recently begun to be produced in Assam, production is still restricted to individual homes.*
Opposite, bottom: *This Kabui-Naga woman uses a simple cotton gin to separate the seeds from the fiber.*

boo leaves but also for the outspread legs of a woman conceiving or bearing a child. The rainbow, on the other hand, might be likened to the course of the clouds, a school of fish and a river.

The colors used in a given textile are also symbolically significant. In the Tuensang District of Nagaland red signifies the blood of enemies. Red used on a sash or on the scabbard of a dagger stands for the fire used to burn the enemy's village. Blue represents the sky and black the night. Thus a black Naga shawl incorporating a red zigzag pattern and a red border can be interpreted as a nightly head-hunting foray, the red zigzag symbolizing the tortuous path through the jungle. Only a successful head-hunter was entitled to wear a garment bearing such symbolism. Moreover many fabrics are reserved for certain echelons of society, for they indicate the social standing of the person wearing them.

The importance of weaving to the indigenous peoples is illustrated by the proportionately large number of words used to describe the art or anything relating to it. Weaving is the exclusive domain of women—a man who tries to weave will be deprived of his manhood or his luck on the hunt. In some tribes weaving is an honor reserved exclusively for the chief's daughters. In some societies it was common to sacrifice an animal every time a fabric

was completed. Furthermore taboos often involve weaving. After every festival, for instance, a taboo period is imposed on weaving. The same is true following births, miscarriages, unnatural deaths or rituals performed to heal the sick, however then a taboo period is imposed on nearly all handicrafts and sometimes on all villagers. The period can last up to a year.

This explains certain attitudes tribal peoples have toward objects they have made, which are thought to be invested with the spirit—that is, the positive and negative aspects—of the artist. That is why traditional peoples rarely sell their handicraft objects. The *aith*, or the soul, of the artist and wearer, inheres in the object. To sell it would mean to sell a piece of the owner's soul. Tribes that barter with their neighbors have therefore devised rituals to purge objects of any negative aspects of the artist's soul. They offer sacrifices to the gods and ask that the acquired fabric be blessed, whereupon they drape it over a dog, which is thought to absorb the negative energy. Likewise a person selling a piece of jewelry first washes it thoroughly so that as little of his soul as possible remains on it. When selling a piece of cloth the weaver removes a thread from the fabric when handing it over to the buyer, a symbolic act of withholding one's own soul.[2]

Above: For the Adis of Arunachal Pradesh weaving and building bridges has the same mythological origin. Their bridges, which have made it possible for them to cross the numerous rivers that flow through their territory, range from simple foot and pillar bridges to elaborate suspension bridges. The tubular, bamboo construction of the latter is particularly striking. The largest of these bridges spans 240 m.

Opposite, left and above:
In addition to the women's simple yet beautiful galle skirts, the men's headdresses reveal the Adis' heightened aesthetic sense. The heavy cane headgears, which are sometimes used as a helmet, come in a wide variety of shapes and sizes. They are decorated with boar's teeth, feathers and beaks of the Indian hornbill, deer's antlers, goat's hair dyed red and black palm fibers. Men adorn themselves with the jaws of tigers, and women don semiprecious stones and silver earrings. The traditional belts of Adi women are called beyops. Their brass discs allude to the following myth: "The sun and moon, who were sisters at the beginning of the world, wore skirts of glowing yellow and flaming red. Their enemy, the frog, stole and burned them and the sisters hid themselves in shame. The whole world was dark until the craftsman Bisi-Ada made two beyops to cover their naked bodies. Hence the sun came into the sky and it was day. But the moon was still shy, even with her disc, and would come out only at night."

Above: The woven articles of Digaru-Mishmi women are particularly fine. Their textiles incorporate motifs symbolizing their worldview. The Digaru-Mishmis live in the valley and mountains of the Lohit District in Arunachal Pradesh.

Above left, from top to bottom: *Two Nocte sashes bearing depictions of human figures. A Nocte loincloth with ornate beadwork. A Tutsa wearing traditional cane rings around his waist and ivory rings on his arms.*
Photograph second from top: A. Nath.

Above: *A Tutsa boy dressed up to perform the Pongtu dance. He is adorned with cut conch shells, cane and metal rings—among them those wrapped in goat's hair dyed black, yellow and red (traditionally these were made from human hair)— and a sash made from red, black and yellow bands to which a cane basket is attached.*

Above: *A Tripuran Jamatia woman at her portable loom.*

Above right, from top to bottom: *The decline of tradition in the Wancho community: the chief's wife wears the head-hunting necklace that, in former times, only her husband would have been entitled to wear, for it indicates the number of heads he has taken. To emphasize her royal status she also adorns herself with a chain of old Indian rupees.*
Ritual ornaments of an Adi miri—a dance and chant leader. Buttons adorn the tiger jaw attached to the
strap of his dao, a machete. Small bells enhance the sound of his rhythmic steps.
Necklaces of a Padam-Adi woman, worn over a traditional tunic.
Nishing woman's belts made from Tibetan bells and beautiful brass and iron discs.
Photographs: A. Nath.

Above: *A Konyak-Naga boy dressed for the Aoling harvest festival held in the village of Wakching.*
Photograph: H. Sanghvi.
Top left: *Adornments of a Tutsa girl.*
Top right: *A Wancho man wearing two sashes, one of which is made from beads, and a bead necklace with three brass heads and fishtails, which, like seashells, are popular fertility symbols.*
Bottom left: *Necklaces worn by a Hill Miri woman, consisting of large beads made from conch shells, blue porcelain, glass and stone.*
Photograph: A. Nath
Bottom right: *The coarse tunic of a Monpa woman, held in place with a beautiful belt. The traditional coral necklace contrasts with the plastic beads purchased at a local bazaar.*

Above: "Shaphi Lanphi," a Manipuri king's shawl, which, in former times, was given by Meithei rulers to favored Naga chiefs to honor acts of bravery and loyalty. One of the last remaining craftswomen in Manipur who is capable of producing this intricate embroidery is Imphal's Meisnam Keinahan Devi.

Top left: *Detail of a Khasi man's frock embroidered with dark blue, yellow, red and green silk. The sash made from silver pieces holds the sheath of his sword.*

Top right: *A Sherdukpen jacket bearing the jana flower motif, horses and the "Chinese fence." Similar jackets, in yellow, red and green, are worn by the Monpas, the Akas, the Mijis and the Khowas.*

Bottom: *The weaving patterns of the Tripuran Chak-mas are particularly fine. Pieces such as these take months to complete.*

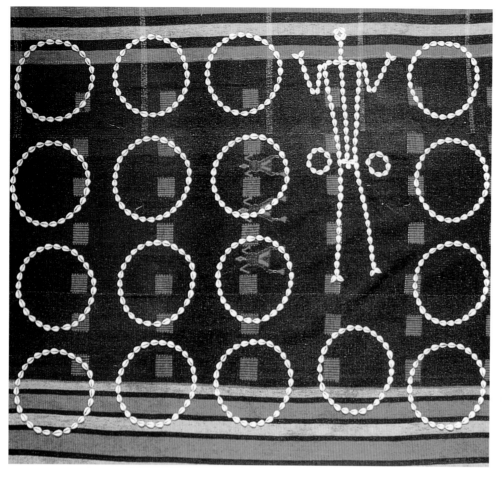

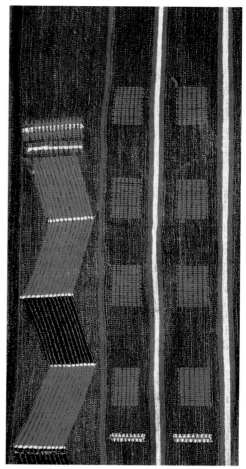

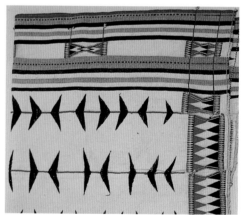

Top, left: *Garment of the Sema-Nagas, adorned with cowry shells arranged in the form of a human figure and circles. The red squares are made from dog hair and symbolize villages that have been raided. Such a garment was reserved for the exclusive use of a successful head-hunter who had given an entire series of feasts of merit.*

Top, right: *Chang-Naga head-hunter's garment. The red-and-black zigzag pattern and red border symbolize nightly head-hunting raids and the tortuous path taken through the jungle.*

Bottom, left: *A beautiful Ao-Naga warrior shawl, or Tsungkotepsu, whose central band bears depictions of mithan buffaloes (signifying the owner's wealth), human figures (representing his prowess in head-hunting), elephants, tigers and lions (symbolizing his bravery) as well as cocks, daggers and spears (signifying his virility).*

Bottom right: *Zemi-Naga garment. The triangles are stylized buffalo horns symbolizing fertility.*

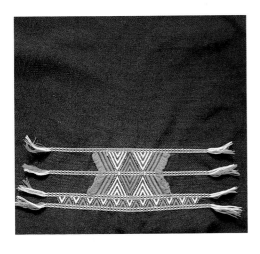

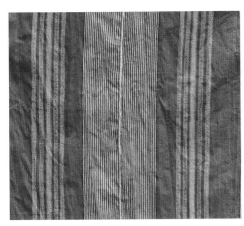
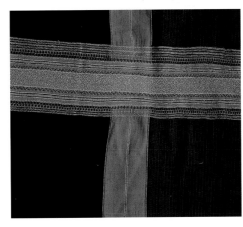

Top: *The embroidery found on the back of a Padam-Adi man's tunic.* Center: *Molsum-Halam woman's skirt.* Bottom: *Jamatia shawl, the figurative embroidery depicting human beings.*

Top: *Apa Tani woman's festival shawl.* Center: *Chakma skirt.* Bottom: *Mizo bag.*

Top: *Nishi woman's garmen, worn on festive occasions.* Center: *Meithei woman's skirt.* Bottom: *Mizo skirt worn at festivals.*

7 ALL IS COLOR AND MOTION

THE WORLD AS A DANCE

Happy and beautiful were the seven virgin daughters of Sun and Moon. One day, at the year's greatest festival, they came down to dance with the village maidens. Reaching the festivity ground they all started turning in circles. Dancing and turning they soon were drunk with pleasure. Dancing and turning the girls, with the boys at the drums, were carried into the sky, swept up as if a hawk had snatched them away. Dancing and turning in the sky they came to the Cloud God, who was so delighted when he saw their dance that he would not let them return to earth. He said to the girls: 'From now on when I send down rain upon the earth, you must dance across the sky and the boys must beat their drums!' He called the girls lightning and the boys thunder. . . . (Tangkhul)[1]

The various dance traditions of the Northeast Indian peoples are united by common functions and motivations. Compelled to dance by certain cues or stimuli, the dancers perform within an overriding framework of inherited and instinctively assimilated principles, which have never been written down or otherwise

The Mogh community of Rupaichari village Tripura performing the candle dance in which the dancers are arranged in a circle and personify the forces of the cosmos.

communicated. It is what has always been "in their blood."

Many ceremonies incorporating dance relate to birth, marriage or death, as well as rites of passage, initiation, betrothal and ancestor worship, all of which are of the utmost importance to the family and the community at large. The attendant emotions find expression in dance. Joy, an emotion known to all human beings, is expressed most readily and spontaneously in dance. Festivals and celebrations that call for the participation of the entire community frequently involve dancing, which playfully promotes and strengthens social cohesion. Love is a primal passion of the human heart of which courtship dances are born. Although these allow free mixing of the sexes, providing a welcome if temporary reprieve from social taboos, they carry no sexual overtones. Erotic songs, however, are relatively common, as are those about legendary lovers. Frequently mirrored in dance is the community's dependence on nature. A bumper crop, which ensures the survival of the village, calls for rejoicing, which is expressed through dance. The growth of crops is thought to be fostered by performing rain rites or invoking fertility spirits. Some dances suggest everyday tasks, such as planting, winnowing and fishing, or occupational activities, such as rowing a boat, pounding the earth, crushing grain or casting a net.

Another function of dance in tribal communities is to dispel shared fears. The *taapu*

of the Minyongs, the sword dances of the Meitheis and various head-hunting dances of the Nagas, for example, serve to relieve the constant fear of territorial war. The anxiety and anticipation evoked by a staged battle, be it one of defense or attack, prepares villagers for war, both mentally and physically.

The indigenous peoples personify natural phenomena in their dances to revere them, to understand them, to strip them of their terrifying qualities, to have power over them. Dancers emulate the movements of such animals as butterflies (the Boros in Assam) and the hornbill (the Kukis in Tripura, the Apa Tanis in Arunachal Pradesh). Other means of portraying animals include using make-up, disguises, costumes or dummies, as in the yak dance and other pantomime dances of the Buddhist peoples of Arunachal Pradesh. Many of these almost ritualistic dances reveal several levels of symbolism, which convey moralizing messages to the spectators. Despite, or perhaps owing to, the seriousness with which these dances are performed, they never fail to contain comic elements, such as amusing masks or men dressed up in women's costumes, which are intended to add levity to an otherwise symbolically laden set of events in which every move signifies something. In folk dance the moves executed by the dancers are simple yet elegant. The hands perform graceful acts of reverence, such as picking flowers or offering food. Occasionally dancers clap their hands or

snap their fingers to the rhythm of the dance or make circular movements with their arms while sitting, kneeling, crouching, standing or jumping. Rarely do dancers perform singly. Instead all dance together, synchronizing their every move. The peoples of Northeast India are renowned for their acrobatic dances, such as the *hozaigiri* of the Reangs in Tripura, in which such objects as pots, bottles, poles, trays and plates are balanced or thrown into the air. In Mizoram the rhythm of the *cheraw*, or bamboo dance, is beat with bamboo poles while dancers move in perfect unison, serving as a visual metaphor for the unity of the entire community.

Also intended to strengthen the cohesion and identity of the community are the dances of the Adis in Arunachal Pradesh, in which members of the older generation recite the genealogy of the tribe for hours on end, going as far back as the days of Abotani the first man. At social and religious festivals tribal history acquires special meaning, and is recited as a rhapsody (*abang*) by a presenter (*miri*). The *miri* is supported by a choir of women, who repeat the verses while dancing to them. These so-called *nyitoms* are as diverse as the social occasions on which they are performed and focus primarily on the various agricultural tasks that must be undertaken throughout the year. Most folk dance formations take the form of lines and circles, which mark out the sacred stage and represent the celestial bodies of the sun,

Many tribal dances relate to the agricultural cycle, which is associated with the cycle of life. The purpose of re-enacting agricultural tasks in song and dance is to bring joy to, to appease and to compel the fertility gods who can provide the community with a bountiful harvest. Molsum-Halam, southern Tripura.

Tripuran Mogh women with elaborate hair decorations dancing with parasols in hand, an ancient symbol of the sun and fertility.

moon and earth. A variation of these is the arc, which is often transformed into a serpentine. In another dance the performers may radiate from a central point, later to reconvene at the center. Some peoples have taken this pattern one step further and have transformed it into a complex *mandala* formation (as in the *rasa-lila* in Manipur—see chapter titled "Poetry, Devotion and Strength"). Separate lines of men and women is the most common dance formation. Occasionally men and women appear alternately, thus forming couples within a single line. A forward-moving line consisting of numerous participants often recalls a slow procession.

Some dances are performed in specific locations, which are ritually purified prior to being used. The location may be chosen on account of a certain temple, shrine or its association with a celebrated figure in local lore. Animistic societies perform their dances in "places of power," such as hilltops, the confluence of rivers, clearings in the forest, in front of certain trees or stone formations, on village squares or in front of or inside houses where the shaman has sensed the presence of a deity, a spirit, a demon or an ancestor. Often these places are specially prepared for *non-psychic* spectators by the erection of shrines, cultic images or totems, around which the dancers perform. In traditional societies, dancing is universally recognized as an exercise akin to praying; consequently it is a profound and intense personal and communal experience. The objective is to communicate with either an invoked, supplicated or propitiated deity with a purposefulness that moves the divinity to respond. The response

may be felt immediately or later, when a disease is cured or a harvest is bountiful.

Thus the notion of time is transcended in dance. Dancers are frequently disguised, either as a divinity or as a kindred spirit who offers the deity a place of refuge, facilitating communication. Herein lies the link to magical dances, which incorporate mystical elements that are accessible only to the initiated. Through the power of dance the shaman acts as priest and medicine man, cures the sick and exorcises evil forces. By dancing in a state of ecstasy ordained performers attain the status of oracles, able to receive messages from the spiritual world, assess situations and predict the future. In most ritual dances performers fall into a trance, which is apparent from their progressively frenetic movements, ending in collapse.

Dances performed in a state of ecstasy are not the only means of establishing contact with the spiritual world. In the *shad suk mynsiem*, or dance of the happy hearts, performed by the Khasis of Meghalaya, virgins dance across a large square, surrounded by youths who are thought to protect them from evil spirits by waving yak tails. The girls' postures remain perfectly upright. The only movement is made by their feet, which are "rolled" from heel to toe, and is nearly imperceptible. Thus the impression is created that something is being "soaked up" from the soil. Indeed that is precisely the purpose of the dance: for the maidens to absorb the earth's powers. Owing to the rigid postures of the dancers, these forces are thought to flow directly through the spine into the girls' heads. The girls' half-closed eyes are believed to enable them to keep the energies within them. Later, when they become women and mothers, they will be able to play their role in society—which is to preserve their cultural heritage and to guard their clan from the forces of evil—by drawing on these absorbed powers.[2]

The great shad suk mynsiem *dance performed by the Khasi women of Shillong is characterized by slow, almost imperceptible moves.*

The taapu, or war dance, of the Minyong-Adis is traced back to Abotani, the first man, who performed it to drive away the evil spirits. The Miny-ong-Adis of Yeksi, Siang District, are one of the few remainig communities to perform this dance.

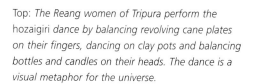

Top: *The Reang women of Tripura perform the* hozaigiri *dance by balancing revolving cane plates on their fingers, dancing on clay pots and balancing bottles and candles on their heads. The dance is a visual metaphor for the universe.*

Bottom: *Zemi-Nagas performing the bamboo dance in the honour of their essential building material, and the hornbill dance, in which the movements of the hornbill are mimicked and costumes incorporating its feathers are donned.* Photographs: P. Bernard.

Above: *Tutsa drummers of Arunachal Pradesh's Tirap District carrying their instruments to the festival grounds.*

Bottom: *Mimicry as a means of assimilating one's environment. Left: A Thadou Kuki woman of Tripura jumping like a hornbill. Right: An Aka boy imitating a rabbit.*

Top: *Martial traditions enacted, practised and anticipated in song and dance: Noctes, Arunachal Pradesh and Thadou Kukis, Tripura*

The Bengali refugees of Tripura enacting the epic of Shiva and Parvati in dance. The strained financial circumstances in which many casteless musician families find themselves often leaves them no choice but to allow their children to take part in these performances. Dressed up like the sacred couple, the children entertain the villagers and bring the stories of the Hindu epics to remote tribal villages.

Dance traditions in Mizoram.

Top: *A war dance of the Hmar clan.*
Left center: *A circle dance of the Lushais.*

Bottom left, above and opposite: *The impressive cheraw, or bamboo dance, in which the forces of the universe are personified and the bonds between members of the community are strengthened.*

...ne dance traditions of the West Kameng and Tawang Districts of Arunachal Pradesh.

Opposite, top left: *In their colorful cham dances the Monpa and Sherdukpen monks personify the entire pantheon of Tibetan Buddhism.* Photograph: A. Nath

Opposite: *As one of the few regions of the Tibetan world the Tawang District has preserved and maintained the ajilamu tradition. This musical drama was composed by Mahasiddha Thang Tong Gyalpo in the 15th century and tells the story of two queens from Lhasa, who are captured by two demons. The king sets out to free them and eventually succeeds by forgiving and befriending the demons.*

Right: *The Akas are known for their festive, colorful dances.*

Poetry, Devotion and Strength

The Art of the Manipuri Dances

Dance is the expression of the primal spark that sets the universe in motion. (N. Levine)[1]

Manipuri, one of four distinct schools of classical Indian dance and certainly the least known, is unique among the various dance traditions of Northeast India. Its incorporation of ancient rituals and subject matter drawn from Indian literature has given rise to an exceedingly rich dance heritage. As in other Northeast Indian societies, the original religion of Manipur's dominant population, the Meitheis, was characterized by numerous animistic cults in which primal gods, mythical heroes and ancestors were worshipped. Since time immemorial this religion has found expression in ritual community dances. In the sixth century A.D. the Tantric magical practices of Assamese Hindus found their way into the "Land of Gems," where they were assimilated into the preexisting religion. In the 15th century the ancient deities of the Sun (Sanamahi) and the Moon (Pakhangba) became identified with those of Shiva and the Snake kings, as well as with Vaishnavite cults. Even today an effigy of Sanamahi is displayed in the southwestern corner of every Meithei household. Moreover the Moon-Snake goddess,

Opposite and following page: The pung-cholom, or drum dance, of Manipur is performed by as many as 100 drummers, whose graceful and expressive movements and rhythms are deftly synchronized.

Pakhangba, is still the main deity of Manipur's royal family. Thus the religious life of the Meitheis is marked by three traditions—animism, Tantrism and Vaishnavism. Likewise elements of all three are to be found in the *manipuri* dance tradition.

The basis of all Manipuri dance is *lai-haroba* ("festival of the gods"), a dance ceremony performed in April, dedicated to more than 500 village deities. At the beginning of the performance spectators are invited by means of gracious hand gestures of the *maibis* (high priestesses) to attend the ceremony. Dressed in white (symbolizing absolute goodness), the *maibis* dance in an abstract formation, which eventually takes the form of a coiled serpent, symbolizing the ancient Moon goddess, Pakhangba. The deity that has been evoked often takes possession of one of the *maibis*, speaking through her to foretell the future.

The typical characteristics of all *manipuri* dances may already be seen in the maibis' flowing movements, which are devoid of sudden transitions and abrupt, exaggerated or angular postures. The dancers' bodies dissolve from one posture into the next. The act of touching the ground by a slight toe movement and the soft, wavelike body movements in the form of a figure eight (the number of eternity) are accompanied by solemn, merely suggestive facial expressions. This typical manner of moving has its roots in folk dance. Although *manpuri* appears to be simple, it is in fact an intricate series of complex movements. Since virtually

all the inhabitants of Manipur dance themselves and are familiar with the dramatic content of the dances, the audience often spontaneously interacts with the performers, revealing the force with which it expresses the intense and fervent religious devotion of the people.

The initial dances are followed by further rituals, which are performed in the mornings and evenings, for as long as 30 successive days. In them flowers are offered; ethical behavior is praised; the world is symbolically re-created by the nine gods and seven goddesses by means of 364 *mudras*, or hand gestures; the human body is symbolically re-created in 64 *mudras*; the various stages of childbirth are reenacted in 40 *mudra* sequences; houses are built; amorous liaisons are acted out; cotton is cultivated; cloth is woven; fish are caught; the dance of the Moon is performed; ceremonial objects are deposited in the temple; a lullaby is sung to put the deities to sleep; and ritual objects are buried near the temple.

The prologue of the great Manipuri drama *rasa-lila* is the *pung-cholom*, or drum dance, which is a kind of *sankirtan*, or communal prayer, and is performed on a number of holidays, as well as on other special occasions, such as the first time an infant is fed solid food, during the piercing of an infant's earlobes, initiation rites, marriage ceremonies, deaths or the anniversary of a death. The *pung-cholom* ranks among India's most impressive and exciting drum

ceremonies. The repertoire of movements of the drum dancer, who cavorts and jumps to the beat of his drum, is virtually inexhaustible. While playing the drum, which produces an astonishingly wide variety of sounds, the performer swings it from the front to the back of his body, lets it circle around him and slings it over his head. Even his head and hair move to the rhythm. Toward the end of the increasingly ecstatic performance the drummer performs acrobatic jumps and spiral movements. These require an extraordinary sense of balance and rhythm. The difficulty of the *pung-cholom* is compounded by the fact that it is a communal dance, performed by a group ranging from two participants to one hundred.

The *pung-cholom*, in which the drummers personify natural phenomena, such as the drizzle of rain, the rolling of thunder or the movements of birds, sets the stage for Manipur's great dance drama—the *rasa-lila*, or sacred circle. *Rasa-lila* performances take place only on the first full moon of a given season. The first performance is always held in the Govindaji temple in Manipur's capital, Imphal, the most sacred shrine in the state. Only thereafter may the dramas be performed elsewhere. The dancing commences at sunset and is brought to a close at sunrise. Five days before the performance the participants, that is the priests, the dancers and their families, prepare the sacred compound that will house the event by building a stage, cleaning the grounds, setting out straw mats for the audience, reciting prayers and chanting sacred songs. The excitement of the dancers and the spectators, who arrive as early as two days prior to the event, culminates on the night of the performance.

There are several types of *rasa-lila*, each variant of which is broken down into five

Top right: *A long procession of priests, musicians and dancers marks the beginning of the Holi festival in Imphal.*
Center: *The Holi festival, in front of Imphal's Shri Shri-Govindaji temple.*
Bottom left: *Meithei temple musicians blowing on conch shells.*
Bottom right: *Stone on display in the State Museum of Mizoram, Aizawl, bearing an ancient Meithei inscription and a depiction of the ancient Moon-Snake fertility goddess, Pakhangba. The serpentine shape of the snake is traced by the* lai haroba *dancers at the end of the ceremony.*

parts. This is perhaps best illustrated by the *vasant* (spring) *rasa*, which begins with:

1) an invocation and a prayer, followed by
2) the sacred *rasa* formation,
3) the initial dance of the main characters,
4) the main drama and
5) the final rituals, which include making offerings and saying prayers.

It recounts the story of the Hindu god Krishna, the most celebrated incarnation of Vishnu, worshipped as the protector and preserver of the world, and his shepherd-esses, the *gopis*. The spectators identify themselves with the *gopis*, who symbolize undying devotion to Krishna. It is not uncommon for men and women to shed tears of happiness during the performance, in which all-pervading love and the sacred truth are conveyed by the participants. The dancers' movements are slow and tranquil. They seem almost transcendent in their stiff, full-length satin skirts, which leave the dancers' feet unseen, thus creating the illusion that they do not move about of their own accord but are impelled by a higher power. Accompanying the dance are inspirational songs, which are sung with great pathos.

The choreography of the *rasa-lila* traces the ancient form of a *mandala*, a series of concentric circles and squares that define a center through their arrangement along the four cardinal points. It symbolizes not only the macrocosms of earth and the universe but also the microcosm of human life. The performances of *rasa-lila* are structured entirely according to this concept: not only do the dancers recall simple *mandalas*, with their circular skirts and their heads at the center (when viewed from above), but also the circular arrangement of the dancers within an area defined by the temple's four outermost poles symbolize a *mandala*, as does the annual repetition of the perform-ances since their inception on the vernal full moon of 1779, inaugurated by Manipur's highest priest. This unbroken cycle is, in turn, analogous to the earth's orbit around the sun. Likewise, the rotation of the earth is implied in the daily rituals performed in the name of Krishna. The time of the performance, between sunset and sunrise, also serves to remind participants of the earth's rotation. Moreover the sacred songs that accompany the drama take the form of

a metric cycle, called a *tala*. The most characteristic feature of this cycle is that it recurs in the same pattern throughout the duration of the performance. The steady movement of the dancers emerging from and returning to the center of the *mandala* is a visual metaphor for the *tala*. The Meithei word for dance is *jagoi*, which means "to turn" or "to spin," revealing that circular movement is a key aspect of Manipuri dance. Certainly the spinning dancers appear to transcend space and time. From its purify-ing function to the intense sensual and

aesthetic pleasure it brings the spectators, *rasa-lila* is a divine cosmic experience in which luminous bodies revolving around a blazing center are recalled. Indeed the *rasa-lila*, the *mandala* in motion, lends its geo-metric shape the divine life force that it represents.[2]

Top left: *The rasa-lila dance.*

Top right: *The* Kunja-rasa *in the Shri Shri-Govindaji temple, Imphal, performed during a full moon in October. The circular formation of the dance is clearly discernible. Photograph: P. Shah.*

Right center: *The Gopa-rasa, performed exclusively by children, in the Shri Shri-Govindaji temple, Imphal, on the eighth day of November. In it the childhood deeds of Krishna are reenacted. Photograph: P. Shah.*

Bottom right: *A Meithei* maibi *opening the lai-haroba ceremony.*

Bottom left: *A Lai-haroba sequence.*

Opposite: *Krishna and Radha, the sacred couple, portrayed by children performing the* Nitya-rasa *in a village temple. In this story Krishna is challenged by Radha and the gopis to perform his most difficult dance steps. Photograph: P. Shah.*

9 WORDS OF THE SHAMAN IN A JUNGLE OF SPIRITS

In the beginning of creation man and spirit were alike. Later, when man beat the spirit frequently, the spirit complained, 'If man keeps beating me the way he does, he will kill me very soon.' God told the spirit: 'If you make some yeast cakes and put black peppers in them and throw the whole lot into the man's drinking well, then, when the man drinks from that well, it will make his eyes black and he won't be able to see you or strike you any more.' The spirit acted just as God had told him to. And when the man tasted the water the following day, his eyes turned black and he was unable to see the spirit, making it impossible for him to beat him. That's why man is no longer able to see the spirit. (Angami)[1]

The myth above explains why man is unable to see spirits; it does not claim that they do not exist. Indeed in Northeast India the world is believed to be full of spirits. For the inhabitants of this region every tree, shrub, hillock or body of water harbors a spirit or a demon. All natural phenomena, such as thunderstorms, rain or wind, are thought to be caused by spirits. Illnesses, too, are attributed to supernatural, usually demonic, forces. This animistic and

A child is being blessed with a leaf by the shaman of the Garo village Chidaogre, Meghalanya.

pantheistic attitude is integral to the mentality of Northeast Indians. Man is considered to be an integrated part of this animated nature. By means of reasoning he is capable of entering this supernatural world. He understands its magical properties and uses them for his own purposes. By instituting the shaman, the peoples of Northeast India created an expert who is able to establish direct contact with spiritual beings. This becomes necessary when an imbalance arises in the world. Such shamanistic insight into the world's interrelations and the ability to make direct contact with these forces distinguishes man from his fellow earthly creatures. With wise foresight and out of respect for nature, man does not take advantage of his position, for he is aware that in due time this would turn against him. The main function of the shaman is to appease the spirits who are the driving forces behind natural phenomena and to use his knowledge of the "invisible world" to make amends with the powers that be, redressing the natural balance.

Thus man does not view himself as standing outside nature, but as being dependent upon it. Illnesses and natural disasters provide ample, if painful, evidence of this fact. Such incidents instill a strong sense of humility in the native inhabitants. By using the powers of the shaman, man tries to make amends for his shortcomings. The shaman falls into a deep trance and, by contacting the spirit world, determines what

man has done to offend the gods. In so doing he uses a language that is usually understood only by himself and his assistant. On returning from the spirit world the shaman gives instructions to the inquirer with regard to cures or rituals to be performed. Northeast Indian shamans usually require that some sort of sacrifice be made, which is of great psychological importance, for it is at once an act of personal distancing, relinquishment and devotion. A sacrifice might entail the slaughtering of an animal, the erection of stone piles, the giving of feasts of merit or the observance of a certain taboo period, which serves to remind man of his dependence on nature. The state of mind induced by such acts creates the appropriate psychological climate for change.

However the shaman also acts preventatively. He is responsible for performing numerous rituals on certain occasions to give thanks for the community's well-being. Such rituals include the life and seasonal cycles of individuals, the community and the environment. In former times the Gallong-Adis of Arunachal Pradesh had a custom called the *neppe nyida*, or "womb marriage," in which the shaman (*nyibu*) chose the future spouse of a child immediately after it was conceived.[2] Chakma women from Tripura are required to observe a number of taboos during pregnancy. On their joints they wear strings made by their medicine men (*vaidyas*), for example, which are believed to ward off evil spirits.

Moreover they are not supposed to answer calls from outside at night, even if the voice sounds familiar to them. They must be careful not to walk past certain trees or the houses of widows.[3] Nocte women in Arunachal Pradesh must remain on a special diet while pregnant. They are not allowed to kill animals or to touch dead persons. Idu-Mishmi women are generally forbidden to eat mithan buffalo meat because it is believed to cause infertility. Tibetan women are not permitted to set eyes on infertile women.[4] Moreover, among many tribes, pregnant women are not permitted to receive guests because they could be accompanied by evil forces. This superstition has reached an extreme level among the Poerah-Tangsas of Arunachal Pradesh, who, for apotropaic purposes, fence in entire houses with high bamboo poles shortly after a child has been born. Furthermore, the Tangsa peoples perform a number of prenatal rituals that are thought to ease childbirth and to ensure a healthy child. Morang-Tangsa husbands perform a ritual in the jungle when their wives are in the fourth month of pregnancy, whereby they lay out piles of rice and sacrifice a chicken

and a pig. The pig's blood is sprinkled on a post that is erected to the left of the entrance of the house, whereas its head is hung above the bed of the pregnant woman.[5] Furthermore, in the seventh month of pregnancy, a dog is tied to a *pipal* tree while a pig is slaughtered inside the house, whereupon the meat is distributed among relatives and friends.

Yet in most animistic societies the shaman's activities begin after the delivery of a child. The Apa Tanis call on a shaman to recite prayers, for they believe that newborn infants are possessed by a spirit (*ui*), which decides their fate and therefore must be conciliated.[6] In many indigenous societies the shaman names the child. The Singpho *dumsawa* gives two names to the newborn, after sacrificing a pig in honor of the ancestor's spirit (*natgoon*), to ensure its favorable disposition toward the child. One of the names remains a secret (*natming*) and is revealed only to the father. This name is closely linked to the child's future, which is read by the *dumsawa* from a pig's liver. Many peoples perform special rituals with a child's first bath water and there are a number of rules concerning the cutting of the umbilical cord with a bamboo knife and the disposal of the placenta. The Minyong-Adis call on the shaman four days after delivery to bless the child in a ceremony in which its head is shaved and earlobes pierced (*dumit nginam*). Similarly four days after delivery the Sherdukpens carry their babies outside to show them to the sun. Two months after birth Pailibo-Adi parents have the *nyibu* foretell the child's future by examining the intestines of sacrificed pigs and hens. These and other oracle practices, such as reading piles of rice or strips of bamboo, are widespread among the peoples of Northeast India.[7]

A special ritual performed to identify interrelations that may help explain certain events is the egg oracle of the Khasis of Meghalaya. The shaman is believed to establish direct contact with the primal mothers. While asking the ancestors why a certain sickness was brought on, for example, he dyes an egg red. The answers to his questions can be read from the location and way in which the eggshells land on the ground after the egg is thrown into the air. The Khasis also contact the ancestors and the primal mother, Ka Blei, in private, for instance, when healing the sick. If someone has fallen ill, the entire clan gathers together, including those members

who live further afield, and recount their creation myth as well as the genealogies of individual families. In this way the sick person is made to feel how important his or her recovery is for the continuation of the family tradition of which he or she is an indispensable part. Since all who are present firmly believe in the healing powers of the spoken word, the patient is sometimes able to muster psychological strength from this support, which may indeed help cure whatever illness he or she is suffering from.[8]

The most important person in the religious life of the Khasis is the *Syiem sad*, or high priestess, from the village of Smit, which lies south of Meghalaya 's capital, Shillong. She wields worldly as well as spiritual power and resides in the last "woman's house" of Meghalaya. At the center of her dark, "sacred realm" is an oak pole believed to be the center of the earth, recalling the oak tree on Mount Sohpetbneng (see chapter titled "Women's Mysterious Realm"). This highest of female shamans is consulted on the fate of the entire Khasi people (in former times on questions of war, for example), determines the dates of important Khasi ceremonies, appoints individuals to the state's most important political positions and even advises people on personal matters. She is arguably the most powerful shaman in Northeast India. Furthermore shamanism is not exclusively a male domain among other Northeast Indian peoples. The Pasi- and Tangam-Adis, as well as many Tangsa groups, have female shamans who act as oracles and judges, prescribe medicine and exorcise spirits.[9]

The members of all indigenous communities solicit the shaman's services, for ritual ceremonies must continually be performed, be it when a girl begins to menstruate, a youth reaches adulthood (such as among the Nagas),[10] a couple marries or a member of the community dies. To secure the blessings of the spirits, animals are sacrificed (chicken, pigs, mithans), from whose intestines the future of an individual or a couple can be divined.

Burial rites enjoy a special status in the ceremonial life of Northeast Indian societies and vary from people to people. The time and circumstances of death determine the appropriate ritual. The shaman often ascertains these by analyzing the intestines of an animal. Many peoples lay their dead out inside the home for relatives to pay their final respects. The Tangsas in

Arunachal Pradesh's Changlang District stridently announce the death of old people by firing rifles, whereas young people who have died of unnatural causes are buried in complete silence, without performing any rituals. Funerals are usually held in the early morning. The Adi peoples, who also bury their dead, tie the hands of those who have died of unnatural causes and immediately bury them where they were found for fear of the person's soul becoming restless and returning as a harmful spirit. Under similar circumstances the Lungri-Tangsas wrap the deceased in thorny shrubs. The Tangam-Adis cover their dead with a shroud. The sons of the deceased carry the corpse in a basket to the burial grounds, just outside the village. They must ensure that, on his or her last earthly journey, the dead person faces the family house. A mithan or cock is sacrificed at the grave and the corpse is buried in a sitting position, with hands folded and gaze directed toward the rising sun. If the funeral cannot be held on the day a person has died, a chicken is strung up by the neck next to the corpse, where it is left hanging until the burial is held—a custom intended to appease the spirits.

Many peoples leave food next to the dead, which is thought to provide nourishment for them on their journey to the afterworld. Others bury the personal belongings of the deceased with them. For the Bangnis—a people from Arunachal Pradesh who are related to the Nishis—including the rope with which the deceased had caught mithans is a custom deemed absolutely essential.[11] In Mizo society it used to be considered necessary to sacrifice at least one animal when a member of the community died, for the animal was thought to guide the deceased into the afterworld.[12] The Zakhrings hang garlands from the house of the dead person for the enjoyment of the spirits, the Monpas put a lantern next to the corpse and the Hill Miris place an egg in the hands of the deceased. In contrast to the Tangam-Adis, when the Hill Miris carry a corpse to the burial grounds it faces in the opposite direction of his or her former house, to prevent another death in the family from occurring in the near future.[13]

Cremating the dead is also a common custom among the peoples of Northeast India. The number of pyres (usually seven), the number of ritual revolutions walked around each pyre as well as the direction in which the corpse lies are of the utmost

importance. In Mishmi society cremation is reserved for relatively wealthy clans. However, their dead are buried and left in the ground until the preparations for the final sacrificial feast have been made. Then the dead are exhumed and cremated on uncultivated land. Many peoples, such as the Chakmas and other Buddhist peoples,[14] collect the ashes and the remaining bones and throw them into a body of water or inter them in clan tombs, as is the custom among the Khasis.[15]

The Tibetan Buddhist peoples of Arunachal Pradesh enjoy a rich heritage of funeral rites, which have developed out of their belief in the rebirth of the dead person's consciousness. They believe that, after a person dies, his or her consciousness remains in an intermediate state (*bardo*) for 49 days and that its reincarnation, or attainment of nirvana, can be favorably influenced by the offerings made and prayers recited by the surviving relatives. The body of the deceased is either buried, cremated or crushed and left to the birds. The latter is rather costly, for it requires the presence of a number of priests (*lamas*), who pray for the soul of the deceased while it is carried off to the heavens by vultures.[16]

The Wanchos of southern Arunachal Pradesh still observe many traditional Naga customs, such as displaying the corpses of their clan chiefs inside the house for five to ten days before interring them in the *rook*, a grave adjacent to the house. After a period of between fifteen and twenty days, once the corpse has been cleaned by worms, the chief's head is severed from his body, cleansed and deposited in a clay receptacle, enabling the fertility powers preserved in his head to be passed on to the clan.

The death of an infant or child is regarded by most peoples as a bad omen. Instead of being given a funeral they are carried deep into the jungle or to a high mountaintop, where they are left. The Idu-Mishmis and the Singphos place a dead child in a basket, which they hang from a tree. In contrast the Havi-Tangsas bury dead

Opposite: *Apa Tani shamans (nyibus) wear special cotton coats that have been dyed black and bear elaborate yellow, red, blue and white embroidery. In spring houses are blessed by sprinkling ointment on their walls.* Right: *Nocte shamans from the village of Lapnan performing two divination rituals, the* wasok *(bamboo ritual) and the* wosok *(egg ritual).*

Portrait of the late Khasi high priestess of Smit (top) and her eldest daughter. Contrary to common matrilineal tradition in Khasi society, whereby only the youngest daughter inherits, it is the eldest daughter of the priestess who will be her heir since she has been exposed to her mother's shamanistic knowledge the longest.
Top photograph: T. Ernsting, Bilderberg.

children beneath their houses, directly beneath the parents' bed. If a pregnant Mempa woman dies, the fetus is removed and buried, whereas the woman is cremated. In former times a gruesome fate awaited twins or mentally handicapped children in Nocte society. As their presence was thought to bring bad luck to the entire community, they were not allowed to survive.

Curiously enough, death among some peoples is associated with hunting rituals. Accordingly, in Lungri-Tangsa society, the relatives of someone who has died go hunting or fishing three days later. When they return they clean their houses.[17] A slight variation of this custom is practiced by the Apa Tanis.

The Miju-Mishmis of Arunachal Pradesh's Dibang Valley District have up to five different shamans, each of whom is responsible for a different task. Other peoples have several different shamanistic experts, too—one to perform rituals and dances, one to cure illnesses and occasionally one to exorcise evil spirits (as done by the *nyigres* of the Gallong-Adis).[18]

In Naga society the latter two tasks are undertaken by the same person, for spirits are thought to be the cause of sickness. The Nagas believe that shamans are constantly surrounded by the spirits (Sema: *aghaus*, Angami: *ropfus*) of animals, such as tigers, snakes, mithans and monkeys, and of people. The spirits are believed to possess powers of divination and are thought capable of removing from a body foreign objects that the shaman (*tumumi*) might take advantage of. In the event of illness the *tumumi* is able to determine if the patient has been touched by an evil spirit or if a spirit has "polluted his body." In such instances the female shaman lubricates the afflicted part of the patient's body with an herbal mixture, utters some incantations, massages the spot, presses the skin under which the pain is felt and sucks it with her mouth. In so doing the shaman extracts brown juice, pieces of stone or bits of bone or hair from the patient's body. The former governor of the state of Himachal Pradesh, the Naga Hokishe Sema, reports having undergone such treatment as a child and was thus cured from severe stomachaches. Afterward the *tumumi* told him that an evil spirit had put some stones in his belly while he was playing alone on the road.[19]

Most Northeast Indian peoples have an ambivalent attitude toward shamans. On the one hand they respect them, on the other, they fear them, for they can put a curse on individuals or entire communities. Yet the people have never been completely dependent on the shaman's powers to appease demons and spirits. They are capable of doing what is necessary in simple rituals, such as consecrating a newly built bridge to the water and wind spirits. The people know which spirits they must pray to (in Pangi-Adi society, for example, Hogum causes disease among mithans and Peitpum may be invoked to increase the birthrate of piglets) and which taboos must be imposed on certain occasions (such as postnatal cleansing rituals and the abstinence from certain food when ill). As in other societies, many such taboos were originally imposed for hygienic purposes and have, over time, been endowed with religious significance.[20]

Opposite: *The central pole in the high priestess' house is purported to have originated from the same oak tree that is said to have connected heaven and earth, which the various Khasi clans used to visit each other. It is wrapped in bamboo to signify its sacred status.* Above: *This shal tree in a forest near Udaipur is revered by the Tripuris as the "mother tree," the mother of all trees on earth.* Above right, from top to bottom: *Near the village of Khaspur an Assamese priest performs a ritual to fortify an infant against the evil eye. He has erected a bamboo shrine with eggs, rice and flour.* Photograph: H. Sanghvi.

A Molsum-Halam shaman from Dhuptali, Tripura, lights the candles of the shrine of the forest goddess, Sengra, thus bringing the deity to life for the ensuing dance festival. Among the Mogh people of Tripura only the shaman is entitled to distribute fire for ritual purposes. Here the occasion is a fertility dance.

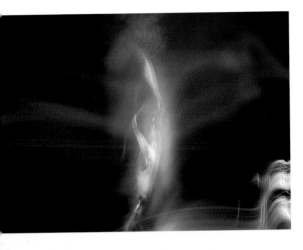

A Garo chief and his assistants performing a divination ceremony with the intestines of a cock. At the same time a child is being "baptized."
Top left, center and bottom: *Before a ceremony can be held at one of the village shrines, several rituals must be performed in the chief's house, during which the participants fall into a trance.* Top center: *The shaman blows into a freshly cut piece of bamboo to attract the attention of the spirit.*
Above: *After blessing the child with a leaf (see p. 94), the shaman presents the sacrifice to the deity, whom the stone at the top of the shrine is believed to embody.*

Afterwards, he passes the cock around the child's head so that the benefits of the sacrifice are directed towards him. Top left: *Since blood must flow to produce an apotropaic effect, the shaman cuts the throat of the cock and smears the blood on the bamboo poles of the shrine.*

Top right: *Afterwards, he removes the intestines of the cock and, based on their shape, foretells the child's future.* Bottom left: *The intestines, through which the cock's feathers are pierced, are affixed to the shrine in the hope that it will be accepted by the hungry spirit as food. The cock is cooked in ginger and eaten by members of the community.* Bottom right: *The child receives final blessings with a leaf covered in the cock's blood.*

Shamanistic rituals among the Apa Tanis:

Right and opposite page, top right: *An Apa Tani shaman celebrates the* korlangui *ritual in a rice field that has been flooded. Its purpose is to appease several spirits, namely Mokum, the soil goddess, who is appealed to for fertility. While reciting magical formulas in the Apa Tani shaman language, the shaman cuts the throats of several chicks at a shrine made from cane and bamboo, which is intended to be an image of the fertility goddess. This spring ritual is performed before the rice cuttings are transplanted. It is followed by two days of ritual abstinence.*

Opposite page, bottom left: *Two shamans performing a fertility ritual at the large shrine (*nago*) near the village of Hang. The shrine consists of dozens of cane structures, symbolizing the entire pantheon of the Apa Tanis. The blessings of the gods are invoked by offering eggs and sacrificing fowl and mithans.*

Opposite page, far left, top and bottom: *Among the Apa Tanis fecund fields are equally as important as fertility among men and women. For this reason shamans are invited by the families to distribute Mokum's blessings. One way to receive this blessing is to build altarlike cane structures on which fowl are sacrificed and eggs offered to the gods. Similar practices are common throughout Arunachal Pradesh. Bottom left photograph: G. Horter.*

Far left top and bottom: *As a sign of his ability to communicate with the spirit world and his unique position in society, the Idu-Mishmi shaman in Aohali, Arunachal Pradesh, wears a pleated black, white, red and yellow woman's skirt, adorned with a sash of assorted tiger, boar and monkey teeth and claws, a bag of bear fur, several ritual daos and a bundle of bells and chimes that accompany him when playing his drum. On his head he wears a band of cowry shells, which symbolizes the universe.* Above: *A Miji priest sacrificing a mithan cow by using his ritual bow and arrow. With a wooden board, to which numerous teeth of various animals, such as tigers, bears and monkeys, are attached, he exorcises an evil spirit from the animal.* Photograph: A. Nath. Left: *A mithan being slaughtered during a Gallong-Adi ceremony.* Photograph: G. Horter.

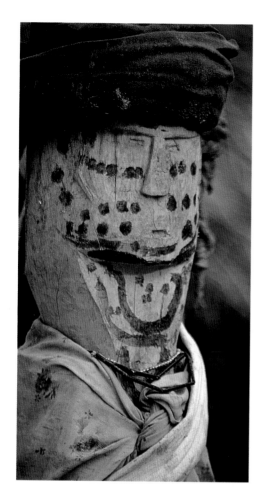

Funeral rites of several peoples:

Top left and right: *The Garos traditionally carve likenesses of the deceased, which are placed in front of his or her house to immortalize him or her.* Bottom right: *In Nocte and Wancho society the personal belongings of the deceased are broken and buried with their owners.*
Center: *The Nocte burial grounds in the village of Laju, Tirap District, Arunachal Pradesh.*
Bottom left: *A Padam-Adi grave.*
Photograph: G. Horter.

Some Wancho and Nocte communities still perform traditional funeral rites, whereby the bodies of the dead, which are wrapped in cotton shrouds, are laid out on elevated platforms surrounded by bamboo fences. Effigies of the deceased bearing his or her tattoo marks are placed in front of the graves. The faceless blue effigies represent deceased women. Bottom left and right photographs: G. Horter.

All the personal belongings of the deceased, his decorations as well as the skulls of the animals he hunted, are put in the grave by relatives, and parasols, which are intended to provide the dead with shade, are stretched out over the effigies (as in the villages of Pongchau, Kheti, Kholam and Laju, Tirap District, Arunachal Pradesh).

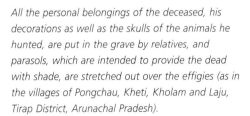

HIGH RELIGION AND MAGICIANS

BUDDHISM BETWEEN TIBET AND BURMA

Follow your path through the magnificent lands that lie ahead of you. You will wander through idyllic places that will seem to you like bits of paradise fallen from heaven. You will pass mountains that shine like precious jewels in the light, and you will cross rivers, whose iridescent foam will remind you of impeccable pearls. Walk through these countries, full of joy and delight, and remember the compassionate omnipotence of Buddhism.
(Rinpungpa)[1]

Scattered along the entire length of the northern boundary of Arunachal Pradesh, in the state's high alpine, alpine and subalpine regions, are the settlements of peoples culturally influenced by Tibetan Buddhism. Ethnically they are divided into the Monpas, the Sherdukpens, the Akas, the Khowas and the Mijis in the Tawang and West Kameng Districts and the Khampas and the Mempas in the Upper Subansiri and Siang Districts. The Mempas also inhabit the Dibang Valley and northern Lohit Districts. The Monpas, which, translated, means "lowlanders" (as opposed to the highlanders of Tibet), form the largest group, with a population of 30,000, and are divided into five subgroups. They consist of skilled traders, cattle breeders and farmers. The territory they

Tawang monastery facing the rising sun on a winter's day. Photograph: A. Dilwali.

inhabit lies between 900 m and 3,600 m above sea level and extends as far as eastern Bhutan, whence their ancestors probably migrated centuries ago. Since the 11th century the cultures of the Buddhist kingdoms of Bhutan, Tibet and Sikkim have heavily influenced that of the Monpas, as is revealed in their clothes (such as *chuba* coats and the Bhutanese-influenced embroidery on women's dresses), dances (for example, such monastic mask dances as the *cham* and the *Ajilamu* tradition, a musical drama), architecture (such as fortified monasteries, or *dzongs*; temples, or *gompas*; symbolic reliquaries, or *chortens*; *mani* walls, built from stacked stones with inscribed prayers; and shrines for prayer drums) and religion. Every village is graced with a monastery inhabited by monks and novices. Moreover the festival calendar is dominated by typical Tibetan Buddhist events, such as *Losar* (the Tibetan New Year), *Chakkar* (a kind of thanksgiving, when the evil of the previous year is warded off) as well as by the festivals of the various Buddhist sects.[2]

The largest Monpa population centers around the Tawang monastery, built in the 17th century. Able to accommodate some 500 monks, it is the largest Buddhist monastery in India. The entire Tawang region occupies an important position in Bhutanese history. Ugyen Zangpo, a member of the influential Bhutanese Nyö clan, migrated to Tawang in the 17th century. One of his sons, Tshangyang

Gyatso, became the sixth Dalai Lama, the theocratic ruler of Tibet from 1683 to 1706. Tawang was also linked to the *shabdrungs*, the "kings of the highest religious power," who were the theocratic rulers of Bhutan from ca. 1650 to 1904. The penultimate ruler in this line, Jigme Dorje, was born here in 1905. However he died under mysterious circumstances in 1931, when he was poisoned. It is presumed that one of the various clans vying for Bhutan's throne murdered the *shabdrung*. In 1911 the Tawang monastery offered asylum to the thirteenth Dalai Lama when he was forced to flee from Chinese Manchu attacks. Finally, in 1959, the fourteenth, and current, Dalai Lama passed through Tawang on his flight into exile, before sojourning in Bomdila, a week's journey on foot further south. Since China's occupation of "Snowland," which led to breaking off all cultural relations with Tibet, Tawang's role has been reduced to the spiritual center of a dozen villages and hamlets as well as numerous nearby monasteries.[3]

Despite the long Buddhist tradition in the Mon region, the Monpas still carry on an older, shamanistic one: after the *lama*, the shaman is still the highest authority in every Monpa village, and the belief in demons and spirits persists here. Accordingly the But-Monpas worship Jo Odi, the mountain god, and sacrifice a large number of animals, such as yaks, chickens and fish, in his name before sowing seeds and after harvesting crops. Like other peoples of

Top left: *Tawang monastery is famous for its library. Its most prized treasure, a Prajnaparamita manuscript written in gold, is displayed in a glass showcase. Behind it is a statue of Manjushri, the god of wisdom. Both are guarded by elephant tusks, traditional good luck symbols.* Bottom left: *Tawang was founded by Mera Lama in the 17th century, during the lifetime of the Great Fifth Dalai Lama (1617–1682).*

Above: *The Gelugpa monastery in Tawang can accommodate some 500 monks. Tawang has always played an important role in the religious life of Tibet. Taxes were paid to the Tibetan capital of Lhasa, which provided financial support to Tawang. Signifying as "holy site founded by a horse," Tawang was the birthplace of the sixth Dalai Lama. This 8-m-high brass statue is of the historic Buddha Shakyamuni and is located behind the main altar of Tawang monastery. The monks' seats are arranged such that their rows lead to the statue, and banners of brocade hang from the pillars and the ceiling.*

The entire monastery has recently been renovated, and most of the older murals have been painted over.

In Tibetan Buddhism masks are an important medium through which spiritual messages are conveyed. The masks represent the entire pantheon of Tibetan Buddhism as well as various aspects of human nature, animals, demons and historic personages. To the devout, the dances are mystery plays in which the moral is often that good triumphs over evil. Just when the play's message becomes too intense the clown Arakacho and his wife appear to add levity to the performance. Photograph bottom right: G. Gessinger.

Ancient animistic symbols are, of course, also hidden in the cham plays performed by the monks of Tawang. Stylistically the masks reveal Tawang's proximity to Bhutan, although local carving styles have also evolved.

Northeast India a But-Monpa bridegroom must pay for his bride by giving her family a yak, two cows and a sheep. Blood relations in But-Monpa society are particularly important. Even today the marriage of cousins (i.e., the daughter of the father's sister and the son of the mother's brother) is deemed the only legitimate form of marriage. Although quite rare these days, polyandry is even practiced in patriarchal Monpa societies, owing to the region's limited availability of land. In this form of society up to three brothers share the same wife—especially in families where the boys have not been admitted to a monastery or do not want to become monks.[4]

South of the Bomdila Mountains, not far from the territory of the Monpas, lie three Sherdukpen villages and numerous Sherdukpen hamlets at elevations ranging from 1,500 m to 2,000 m above sea level. In 1841 the Englishman William Robinson wrote about the region: *Mountains beyond mountains, hurled together in wild confusion, seem to the spectator like the wrecks of a ruined world; and whilst the eye is gratified with the pleasing panorama, a series of hills innumerable is presented to view, retiring far away in fine perspective, till their blue conical summits are relieved by the proud pinnacles of the Himalayas towering their lofty magazines of tempests and snow midway up to the vertex of the sky, and exhibiting scenes calculated to animate the mind with the most sublime sentiments, and to awaken the most lofty recollections.*[5]

Like the Monpas the Sherdukpens build stone houses, whose foundations serve as a shelter for cattle and horses. Owing to the cold climate the houses are almost entirely devoid of windows. The different materials with which they construct their roofs—wood, bamboo and grass—reveal the elevation at which they lie. The Sherdukpens (in Tibetan *sher-druk-pen*, which signifies "The Lords of the Eastern Dragon Country") migrated from Bhutan to West Kameng, to which their language, creation myth and

Left: *Men and women of the Sherdukpens and the Monpas wear round caps of waterproof yak felt (gurdams). The rain flows away from the hat's twisted ends. Like Monpa women, Sherdukpen women don maroon cotton jackets bearing imaginative white, yellow, red and blue embroidery. The silver jewelry originates largely from Tibet and is often fitted with turquoise and other semiprecious stones.*

physical traits bear witness. Their democratic society is split into three classes, which are not strictly segregated. The village council (*jung*) plays an important role in society. It is headed by a *gaonbura*, who is associated with the district administration. Owing to the severe winters, the Sherdukpens migrate south, to the Assam border, in December, where they remain until March, when they return to their homes to begin sowing buckwheat, wheat, barley and rice.[6]

East of the Sherdukpen region lies the territory of the Akas. Various rivers flow through this 200-square-km region, which is part of the subtropical Himalayan foothills with elevations ranging from only 91 m to 183 m. The Assamese word "Aka" means "painted." The name alludes to the Aka women's custom of elaborately painting their faces with a mixture of pine resin and charcoal. The Akas call themselves "Hrusso" and are divided into 11 clans and subclans. In their creation myth they count themselves among the ruling class (see chapter titled "The Indigenous Peoples of Northeast India and their Origins"). Over the centuries the Akas have been influenced by neighboring peoples, for the originally shamanistic and animistic people has, at least on a superficial level, adopted certain Tibetan Buddhist and Hindu concepts.

Their traditional religion personifies natural phenomena: Metz Au is "Father Sky," Phu Au is "Father Mountain," No Ain is "Mother Earth" and Hu Ain is "Mother Water," all of whom are ruled by Tcharo, the "Mild Lord," who also presides over the world of man and beast. Many sacrifices are made in his name, especially before sowing seeds in spring.

Some Aka customs reveal certain cultural affinities with those of other tribes living in the rainforests of Arunachal Pradesh. Like the Nishis, the Apa Tanis and the Adis, Aka men always carry a *dao* with them, a kind of machete, and Aka families used to live in longhouses. These solidly built wooden pile dwellings with straw roofs reached up to 60 m in length and 7 m in width and rested on 2-m-high bamboo poles. The space between the ground and floor of the house served as a shelter, primarily for pigs. The houses, which were equipped with bamboo verandahs on two sides, were divided into three or four rooms, which housed three to four related families. More frequently, however, only the families of two brothers shared a house. Polygamy is also common in Aka society, another aspect of

their culture that unites them with other peoples of Arunachal Pradesh.

Culturally and ethnically related to the Akas, though employing a different language, are the Khowas. In the complicated hierarchy of the various indigenous peoples, the Khowas act as the paid servants of the Akas. In their territory, which includes seven settlements and their environs, the Khowas cultivate maize, millet, wheat, potatoes and several other kinds of vegetable. Also related to the Akas in appearance and customs are the Mijis, who live in 25 villages in the Bichom River Valley, just north of Aka territory. The Miji language is also different from that of the Akas, and their main divinity is Jang lang Nui. In October a great seven-day festival is held in his honor.[7]

The other two Tibetan Buddhist peoples of Arunachal Pradesh, the Khampas and the Mempas, live along the Tibetan border. The proud Khampas, who reside primarily in the Tibetan province of Kham, which extends into the present-day Chinese province of Sichuan, played a key role in defending the region against the Chinese. Referred to as a "people of kings," they were reputed to be fierce warriors, whom even Dshingis Khan could not defeat. They are larger in stature than other Asians, and their pride, courage and ferociousness are legendary.[8] The Mempas, who inhabit the northern Dibang Valley and Lohit Districts, reveal close cultural ties to them. Just like the Khampas, they have assimilated elements of Tibetan Buddhism into their shamanistic religion.

Recalling the olden days in Tibet: Monpas and Sherdukpens sharing chang—beer made from barley. Photograph: A. Nath.

Yet, in their villages, there are no more practitioners of the purely animistic religions. Nonetheless some of the ancient *Bön* cults are still alive. For the peoples living near Bhutan and Tibet, these cults, once widespread in the entire Tibetan realm, still play as central a role as the teachings of the Buddha. The magical practices of their shamans (called *frimpas, phrames, chajee romus, chizes, monpus, cangmeys, givis, phabis* or *mugous*),[9] their bloody sacrificial rituals and their incantations reveal how the

Top: *An Aka shaman in his longhouse next to a pair of buffalo horns, which bear witness to the prevailing animistic tradition in Aka society. His cane hat, or musgera, is adorned with a narrow cloth band or fur, leaves and flowers. To wear such a cockade, from which spikes project, is a privilege reserved exclusively for hunters who have killed a tiger.*

Bottom: *The exterior as well as the interior of Aka houses reveal the shamanistic tradition of this people: cane structures, phallic stone piles and such shaman's weapons as a bow and arrows and ritual daggers.*

ceremonial life in Tibet must have been before the final conversion to Buddhism in the 11th century. The survival of these traditions may be the result of the tolerance embraced by Buddhism, which is not predicated on absolutism. On the other hand these traditions reveal the peoples' cultural affinity with the culture of the lowlanders, who are still in contact with their "original soul."

A comparison of the different forms of Buddhism practiced in the Himalayas shows that the entire Himalayan and sub-Himalayan realm, from Arunachal Pradesh and Bhutan to Sikkim, Nepal and the western Himalayas, including the regions of Ladakh, Lahaul-Spiti and Kinnaur, is dominated by Tantrism (see section on Assam in chapter titled "Women's Mysterious Realm"). Consequently the whole area is often referred to as the "Tantric belt." An examination of the regional variations in the performance of Tantric rituals shows that the further west one looks the more spiritual in nature they become. In Northeast India a sacrifice is performed by slaughtering animals, whereas "sacrifice" in the barren western Himalayas merely signifies a spiritual attitude, which embraces purification rituals, acts of penance and meditation.[10]

Another form of Buddhism is also practiced in Northeast India: Southeast Asian Hinayana Buddhism in its Theravada form. In it the original teachings of the Buddha, who claimed that enlightenment can be attained only through personal effort, are still taught. The peoples of Arunachal Pradesh who practice this form of Buddhism are the Khamptis and the Singphos, who inhabit the lower regions of the state's Lohit and Changlang Districts. They are a branch of the Shan, or Kachin, peoples, who live near the source of the Irrawaddy River in Burma, from whom they separated in the late 18th century on account of tribal feuds. The societies of both these peoples are marked by stringent hierarchy. Until recently blood feuds (*punglat*) were a common means of settling disputes. The family of the perpetrator were absolved only if they were prepared to recompense the murdered person's family properly for their loss: cowry shells for his teeth and nails, swords for his fingers and toes, rifles for his arms, slaves for his legs and gongs for his head and mouth. The reasons for this bloody custom may stem from the peoples' belief in demons and spirits, which was just as

strong as their devotion to Buddhism. In such animistic cults, blood sacrifice played an extremely important role (see chapter titled "I am the Tiger"). The Khamptis and Singphos still venerate the spirits of the family, the clan and the village (*phis* or *nats*).[11]

Such practices are shared by the Buddhist peoples of Tripura, the Moghs and the Chakmas, who live in the hills of that state. Where the Moghs originally came from is uncertain. According to Burmese chronicles, in the sixth century A.D. a Mogh kingdom covered an area that extended from the Meghna Delta and the Chittagong Hills in Bangladesh to Udaipur in the south of Tripura. The Moghs, whose name in Bengali signifies "pirates" (derived from their ruling status on and around the Meghna River in Bangladesh), call themselves "Marmas," which in Arakkanese denotes "Burma." Arakkanese, in turn, is closely related to the Burmese language, but has its own script. Mogh customs and traditions also reveal certain affinities with those of the Burmese. Every village is graced with a small temple (*kheyang*) that is built in the style of the local bamboo architecture, in which monks (*shampuras*) lead a celibate life in the name of Buddha.[12] As in Burma it is customary among the Moghs that every boy between the ages of seven and twenty-one lives in the temple for at least a week, where he is inducted into the life and teachings of the Buddha and becomes a member of the Buddhist community (*sangha*). In a ritual called *sangrubui* the boy's face is painted, he is

Like a fortress, the Tawang monastery is perched atop a 3,048-m-high mountain, near the Tibetan border. Photograph: G. Horter.

dressed in elegant clothes and is carried to the monastery in a magnificent procession, where the *shampura* cuts his hair. Girls also spend a prescribed length of time in the temple before their first menstruation (*rangtanqre*), when each is given a piece of cloth, with which they are supposed to cover the upper part of their bodies henceforth.[13]

The Moghs are known for their sexual equality. Female property remains in female hands. When a woman dies, half of her worldly possessions goes to the eldest daughter, the other half is divided among the other female family members. The tradition of boys' and girls' dormitories, in which adolescents convene but do not spend the night, has survived among the Moghs. Visits between the two houses are frequent; they are where the first romantic ties are formed, which may lead to marriage later. The most important Mogh celebration is the water festival. This occasion attests to the animistic beliefs still held by the Moghs, for its purpose is to honor and appease the water goddess. She is called on to ensure fertility and to protect the community from flooding. The Moghs also venerate the forest goddess, Chichi, whose benevolence or wrath may strike entire households, therefore she must be appeased regularly,

with the help of the shaman (*thangpara*), by sacrificing pigs and fowl.[14]

The culture of the Chakma people, who originally also came from Burma and practice Theravada Buddhism as it is done in the Chittagong Hills of present-day Bangladesh, is also deeply influenced by animism. All celebrations connected with important events, such as birth, marriage, the growth of crops, the acknowledgment of social prestige and death, are performed by Buddhist priests and shamans (*lorhi*). Always accompanied by sacrifices (pigs, goats, cocks and doves) and offerings (rice, vegetables and fruit), Chakma rituals are extremely complex and marked by a fervent desire to secure the gods' acceptance of the sacrifices.

Thus the Chakmas have developed a complicated system that enables them to determine whether or not their sacrifice has been accepted by a given deity. They infer this knowledge from natural clues: for example, in the *vadya puja*, a rite that pays homage to the ancestors, the *lorhi* coaxes the souls of the dead to cross the threshold of death again in order to partake of the food that has been laid out for them. The flies and insects that settle on the food are thought to be the spirits, reborn into lower life forms. In order to expiate the sins of the condemned souls and possibly to ensure a better reincarnation for them, the *lorhi* recites further incantations. The *jadi puja*, which may be performed only in the densest recesses of the jungle, requires solitude and an eerie sylvan semidarkness. It is regarded as a good omen if, shortly after the beginning of the recitation of the magical verses, a faint miasma of smoke rises from the offering, which consists of rice wrapped in a banana leaf. If a spider appears a few minutes later and begins spinning a web around it, the *puja* is thought to have been completely accepted by the deity.[15]

The practices of the Chakmas attest to the process of assimilation to which such Buddhist concepts as reincarnation have been subjected in an animistic context. It would seem that what has been said about the peoples practicing Buddhism along the borders of Bhutan and Tibet also applies to the Theravada Buddhists of Northeast India—that their original animistic spirit will always shine through, no matter how strongly it is overlaid by the so-called world religions, be it Buddhism, Hinduism or Christianity.

Above and opposite bottom: Simple monasteries of the Tripuran Mogh people. This poor community boasts an astonishingly large number of monks. Opposite Top left: Some followers of Theravada Buddhism believe that the Assamese village of Hajo is where the historic Buddha died. Therefore even the Hindu temple has a carving of Shakyamuni. Opposite Top center and right: Religious expressions of the Buddhist lay people of the Mogh community of Tripura. *Prayer flags with millions of mantras fixed to bamboo poles reach up into the sky. A stupa, the highly symbolic Buddhist reliquary shrine made from paper, at the monastery of Rupaichari.*

11

"I AM THE TIGER, THE BUFFALO IS MY SISTER"
MAN, BEAST AND MISSIONARIES IN NORTHEAST INDIA

Buslu-Ao, the first man in the world, had three sons and three daughters. There were no other people in the world, so naturally they had to marry each other. Only Chalo-Michisi, the youngest daughter, was unhappy having to marry her own brother. She refused herself from her husband and declined to work in their household. In this way a whole year went by in constant quarreling until her husband couldn't stand it any longer and beat his wife. Ashamed and miserable she sank down in a corner of the house.

But when the others went to the fields, she got up, took bamboo vessels in her basket and gourds to fill them and went down to the river for water. When she reached it, a strange magic befell her: following an inexplicable impulse she put the basket on her head and placed the gourds on either side as horns; she used the rice-beer strainer as a tail and tied bamboo tubes to her arms and legs. Then she ate her own clothes and this made both her sides swell. In this way she turned into a mithan buffalo and wandered into the jungle, where she remained. Two days passed until the other brothers and sisters began to get

worried and started searching for her. The bumble bee told them of their sister's strange transformation and led them to her. Bursting into tears about Chalo-Michisi's change her husband caught her and led her back to the house. Their father said: "We cannot allow my daughter to wander about in the jungle. We must make proper arrangements for her. I suggest we tie her up near the house." He made a strong rope of cane and tied her to a pillar. They offered her food and water, but she refused to eat or drink; she just stood there weeping. Moved by her tears her father said: "You are my daughter—in fact you're both daughter and daughter-in-law, but the Great Lord has turned you into a mithan. What can we do? Don't carry on like this; you should eat just as we eat.

Then his transformed daughter spoke: "It is true that the Great Lord has turned me into a mithan, and I am quite happy about it, but at the same time I'm a woman and I can't possibly live without a husband. Let me go so that I may find a mate!" When her father heard this he released her and Chalo-Michisi went in search of a suitable husband. She met the dog, but he was too small. More suitable was the pig because his skin was quite like hers. Yet the pig was also too small. The horse and the deer were likewise too different, as well as the

bear, the tiger, the monkey and all the animals of the forest. Exhausted from her long search the human mithan finally came to the place of the rising sun. She crossed the river of cold waters and the river of hot waters, and there at last she found, standing in the sandy bed of the river, a male mithan. She was thrilled by the sight of him. They fell in love and shortly thereafter she bore two calves.

Meanwhile Chalo-Jijao, Chalo-Michisi's human husband, fell ill and the family called the priest to find out what was ailing him. He declared that the boy could be cured only if a mithan were sacrificed. In his vision he viewed the place beyond the river of cold and the river of hot waters, where the mithans were to be found. Sijji-Jao and Machlo-Jao, the two elder brothers, set off to find them and after a long journey finally reached the place of the rising sun. They crossed the river of the cold waters but the heat of the river of the hot waters was unbearable. The clever brothers came up with the trick of luring the mithans with salt and leaves. But only the two calves and the mithan that once was Chalo-Michisi survived the crossing of the river of the hot waters. Tied to thick ropes the two brothers led their mithan sister and her calves home, and again tied them to the pole on the side of the house. Buslu-Ao's wife came out to look at them and, realizing that

A Konyak elder leaning against carvings of a tiger and a mithan buffalo. Photograph: H. Sanghvi.

this was her own daughter, said: "It is true that she once was our daughter, but the gods desire to have her. We will have to sacrifice her." But all their dagger stings and axe strokes could not break the skin of Chalo-Michisi. Finally Buslu-Ao's wife said: "She is our daughter and it's not possible for us to kill her, unless perhaps we tell her that it's her duty to die." Carefully she approached her mithan daughter and whispered in her ear: "When you were a human being, you were my daughter and it would not have been possible to sacrifice you, but now you are a mithan and it is your time to die." She moved aside and the others struck the poor creature with their daos until Chalo-Michisi, the human mithan, was dead... (Aka)[1]

Most of the hill peoples of Arunachal Pradesh, Nagaland and Manipur attribute magical qualities to fauna. To this day the indigenous inhabitants believe that, by slaying an animal, the qualities and powers attributed to it are passed on to the person who killed it. For this reason the hunters of many Northeast Indian peoples adorn themselves and their houses with hunting trophies (tiger jaws and claws, beaks and feathers of the Giant Hornbill, buffalo horns and skulls, monkey skulls and hands), so that the strength of the animal is transferred to them and their household. The future is divined by reading animals'

intestines and animal sacrifice is used to appease the spirits and gods. Among the animals sacrificed the mithan is the most highly revered. Endemic to Northeast India's jungles, mithans (*bos frontalis*) are a cross between a cow and a wild gaur. In the aforementioned Aka myth, the shaman demands the sacrifice of a mithan so that Chalo-Jijao, the human brother and husband of the mithan, a mythical ancestor, can recover from his illness. This reveals the divine qualities with which the ancestors are attributed and how closely the tradition of sacrifice is linked to ancestor worship. To appease the ancestors is to heal, to restore a sense of wholesomeness and the unity of all things. This whole, wholesome or holy state can be brought about only by performing sacrifices involving great personal effort. The sacrifice of a mithan represents such an effort.

In the myth, the hunters, in order to find mithans, must make their way to the place

Above and left: *After catching a mithan buffalo, a Hill Miri man leads it to his village, which will earn him great prestige.*

of the rising sun, where seemingly insurmountable obstacles are encountered (the unfordable rivers of burning hot and ice-cold waters), and a vast and rugged terrain must be crossed. That the transformed Chalo-Michisi is at first unable to find a suitable partner implies that the mithan is unique among animals. The animal's special status is further attested to by its sheer size and strength, qualities that make hunting it even more difficult. Overcoming both factors—the animal's immense strength and the inaccessibility of the terrain it inhabits—leads to the attainment of spiritual power that the sacrifice of a mithan represents and that can bring about the

unity of all things. In Hill Miri society this idea exists in a slightly modified form: the highest gods in the Hill Miri pantheon are the "four brothers as large as mountains." In their dreams, shamans and visionaries travel to the lofty palaces of the gods, a 12-day walk east of the Hill Miri settlements. To reach them they must climb numerous high mountains and ford two rivers. The gods accept only full-grown mithans as proper sacrifices since only the strongest can survive the long and arduous journey. As recompense, only the shaman, who has led the mithan's heavy soul such a great distance, is entitled to keep the animal's magical left shoulder blade once it has been sacrificed.[2]

Owing to the difficulty of the undertaking, a successful mithan hunt is an extremely prestigious affair, attesting to the hunter's courage and strength, hence his virility. That he lures the animals with salt,

thus obviating the need for him to ford the treacherously hot waters, demonstrates his understanding of the natural world and his superior intelligence, which distinguishes man from beast. That the hunter is not permitted to kill the animal when he encounters it, but must lead it back to his village so that his fellow villagers can partake of his success, reveals the prestige associated with the mithan hunt. Yet, owing to the village shaman's ability to communicate with the spirit world, only he is entitled to perform the sacrificial ceremony, ensuring that the potential dangers involved in killing the powerful mithan are avoided and the fertility attributed to the animal benefits the entire community.

During mithan sacrifices among the Sangtam-Nagas, a prayer is said to the god Tsungrangre: "Today we are offering you this mithan. May there be no rain today. May everything go well. May all our men

Panwang Raja, the chief of the Nocte village of Kheti, and the local shaman, in front of his house, which is adorned with buffalo skulls.

and women multiply. Bestow upon us a good harvest."[3] The shaman speaks to the sacrificial animal and secures its "consent" to being sacrificed, recalling the Aka myth. Similar are the practices of the Reangs of Tripura, whose *ojhas* whisper into the animal's ear: "O he-goat, you will be sacrificed today. Your mother and father (the gods, or ancestors, whose spirits animate all beings, including the animal to be sacrificed) provided for this. I am not responsible; neither are my assistants. Do not curse us."[4]

On account of their high status mithans are still used as dowries in Arunachal Pradesh. In addition to other gifts and money,

Top: A Wancho man from the village of Nginu standing next to his clan's totem, a tiger, carved from wood.

Bottom: *In order to acquire the fertility power that mithan skulls are believed to possess, a Zemi-Naga man jumps up to a pair of mithan horns hanging from the ceiling of a morung.* Photograph: P. Bernard

Above: *A Wancho man of Nginu has been advised by the chief to lead a mithan to a neighboring village and offer it as a gift to secure the village's friendship. The rope will be the most important and prestigious item put in the man's grave when he dies, since it attests to his skill as a hunter and, therefore, his fertility power.*

Above: *A former Wancho head-hunter of Nginu performs a fertility dance while wearing his skull bag, which is decorated with monkey skulls and mountain goat horns.*

Top right: *A Tutsa proudly displaying a tiger blanket.*

Center right: *The Nishis and Hill Miris adorn themselves with hunting trophies. Their headdresses, boapa, consist of a plaited cane helmet decorated with the beak and feathers of the Giant Hornbill, chicken claws, bat heads and monkey skulls. The hair is tied in a knot above the forehead and held in place by one or two long brass pins, damlo. A strip of colored cloth, to which feathers are attached, is wound around the knot and a narrow band of braided cane, to which tiny bells are attached, is wrapped around the head. This podum is worn by Nishi men, beginning at the age of 16. Photograph: G. Horter.*

Bottom right: *Feathers and monkey tails are used to ward off evil spirits at the entrance of Mizo houses.*

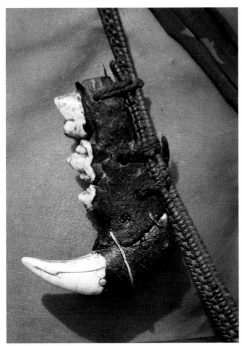

Top: *Tiger teeth of Panwang Raja, the chief of the Nocte village of Kheti, which are sworn by in disputes.*

Bottom: *Half of a tiger jaw, worn by a Tutsa hunter above his traditional cane rings.*

five mithan bulls are given to the bride's father as payment. No sum of money or other gifts to an equal value may be given in place of the mithans for, traditionally (in Aka mythology, for example), the only gift commensurate with the loss of a human being (here symbolic of the bride's father giving his daughter away to another man) is the mithan, since sacrificing human beings is no longer a legitimate means of reconciliation. Secondly the bridegroom must prove his virility, hence fertility potency, to his future wife and her family, which money alone cannot do. The possession of mithans raises the status of the family to whom they are given, for they increase the family's chances of being able to hold a huge feast, at which the mithans are sacrificed and many people fed. It also explains why so many peoples of Arunachal Pradesh still practice polygamy. The more wives a man has, the more likely it is that he will have daughters, whose marriage, according to this system, ensures the family prosperity and prestige. This custom is diametrically opposed to that practiced in some echelons of Hindu society, whereby the bride's family is compelled to pay ruinously large dowries to the bridegroom's parents.

Polygamy is fairly widespread in Northeast India for economical reasons, too. Since women are responsible for most of the field and housework, a man is better off taking several wives, provided he can afford it. The varying degrees of status enjoyed by the first and any subsequent wives is revealed in the disproportionately high number of mithans paid for the first wife. Owing to the rapid population growth over the past several decades and the drastically diminished number of mithans, however, this custom has become increasingly less viable. Some peoples in whose areas mithans have become rare have resorted to using pigs instead.

Some of the practices described in the present and following chapter would seem to indicate that, as in many parts of the world, human sacrifice was at one time common among many Northeast Indian

Top and bottom: *The Apa Tanis of Hang village setting off on a ritual hunt. One of their fellow villagers died in an accident the night before. His male friends and relatives have gathered together to hunt the soul of the deceased in order to free it from the inauspicious circumstances under which it died.*

peoples. In light of this the Aka myth may serve to explain how human sacrifice gave way to that of animals—a phylogenetic step deemed by anthropologists to point the way to a higher level of cultural development. It is, after all, a human being that becomes a mithan and is sacrificed. The animal takes on the woman's attributes. When sacrificed, it is thought to die in place of the human being, thus obviating human sacrifice.

The following story illustrates another aspect of the deep tie that binds the peoples of Northeast India to animals:

One day several fairies descended upon the earth to bathe in a pond. When a young Mizo, on his way to the Kut festival, caught sight of them, he hid behind a great oak tree. The fairies dropped their clothes in a pile and got into the water. The young man lunged forward and caught hold of one of the fairy's clothes, who was therefore unable to escape. She appealed to the young man and promised: "I will bestow upon you plenty of deer every day if you so wish, but do not shoot any animal with a white face as I ride on such animals." The young man let go of the garment and the fairy flew away. From that day on the young man had no dearth of animals on the hunt. He was able to shoot hundreds of animals a day. At first it earned him respect among his fellow hunters. Soon, however, he became an object of envy. Alas his growing disgust for the indiscriminate killing and his growing compassion for the animals soon made the Mizo grow tired of such gratuitous slaughtering. He prayed to the fairy to reappear. On hearing that the hunter was exasperated with his gift-cum-curse, she released him from the spell, whereupon the Mizo became a normal hunter again. Too much of anything loses its flavor. . . (Mizo).[5]

The hunter grows tired of his success. Killing more game than required causes the hunt to lose its spiritual meaning. An increasing sense of disgust and compassion for the animals he has killed wells up inside him. He realizes how inextricably he is bound to them.

The relationship between man, animals and spirits is also the foremost subject in Naga religious thought. In their creation myths the Nagas recount that the first man, together with the first spirit and the first tiger, were siblings, born of the same primal

mother. Only a competition between man and tiger reveals the difference between them: intelligence, of which man is more generously endowed than the tiger. A race to an agreed point was to be held to determine which of them was to live in villages and which was destined to roam the jungle. Man allied himself with the spirit, shooting an arrow at the target while the tiger ran toward it. Thus man reached the target first and the furious tiger had no choice but to make the jungle his home.

Similar to the totem cults of Native Americans in the northwestern United States, several Naga peoples have been known to attribute the qualities of certain animals, such as tigers, frogs or dogs, to certain clans. To this day the Idu Mishmis of Arunachal Pradesh strictly prohibit the eating of either tiger or hoolock gibbon meat, for it is believed that man is related to these animals.[6] For the Paites of Mizoram the tiger is believed to be "God's dog." If a chief is unable to resolve a dispute between two parties, he takes out the sacred tiger's tooth and has each party bite it while warning them that if one of them lies before the chief, the tiger will kill him. Thus the tiger is thought capable of extracting the truth and punishing those who have lied to the chief.[7] The Garos believe that the soul of a man killed by a tiger or an elephant is reincarnated in the body of the respective animal, the underlying notion being that the essence of the victim is acquired by the animal.[8] The Angami-Nagas frequently use leopard skins as shields, with the head facing downward; they believe that if the head of the animal is raised above the height of the shield bearer, the soul of the leopard will cause the latter to stumble and fall.[9]

In many indigenous societies it was essential to observe a series of purifying taboos, such as when a man was forced to kill a tiger. The duration of these taboo periods was roughly the same as those observed when a human being was killed. Such taboos are still observed among the peoples of the Siang and Subansiri Districts of Arunachal Pradesh, such as the Adi-Pasis. The Apa Tanis have special "penitents'

Hunting trophies used to ward off evil spirits and to display the prestige of the hunter. Monkey, deer, cow and buffalo skulls still adorn the outside walls of this modern Christianized Mizo household near Aizawl.

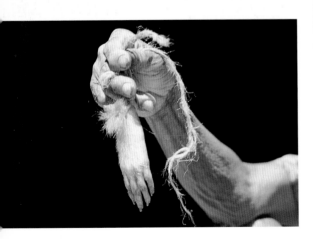

huts," shacks so small that a man is capable of only squatting in them, where offenders must spend prescribed lengths of time. The importance of heeding taboos is already suggested in the last sentence, the moral, of the Mizo story: "Too much of anything loses its flavor." Killing an animal always has a spiritual dimension to it and may be undertaken only in this spirit and if it is accompanied by the necessary rituals. The ensuing taboo period must be observed, without exception; it is the indispensable means by which man may, indeed must, redress the natural balance in order to keep fate from turning against him or his people. If this period of abstinence is not respected, life becomes unhealthy, nature falls into a state of disequilibrium and is no longer sacred, the unity of all things collapses.

These notions are the furthest developed among the Nagas. They believe that man has two, sometimes three, souls: one leaves the body at death, vanishing into the realm of the dead; another remains inside the skull as fertility power (see chapter titled "Fertility through Stones and Heads"); and yet another is an alter ego, the second personality of a person, which large cats are

Opposite, top left: *Assam's Kaziranga National Park is home to a large population of tigers.* Photograph: A. Gomille. Opposite, top right: *The carved symbol of the largest clan of the Tutsa community in the village of Kholam.* Opposite, left center: *The Wanchos still carry on the ancient tradition of hanging honeycombs in the doorways of their houses, for the bee spirits are thought to ward of evil spirits by stinging them.* Opposite, right center: *Mithan skulls displayed atop Y-shaped posts, the traditional symbols of female fertility, which are used in sacrificial ceremonies in a Lushai village in southern Mizoram.* Opposite, bottom left: *A monkey arm held by a former Nocte head-hunter, in the village of Kheti.* Top left: *A Garo nokpante (bachelors' dormitory) richly adorned with tiger carvings.* Top right: *Tiger totem at the Wancho chief's house in the village of Pongchau.* Center right: *A stuffed tiger inside the morung of Longching village.* Photograph: P. Nalin. Bottom right: *Carvings of hornbills, a tiger and a* human couple in Mokokchung's morung. Photograph: P. Nalin. Above left: *An Apa Tani "penitents' hut."* Above right: *"Totem pole" in the morung of the Wancho village of Wakka.* Photograph: G. Horter

hunter, it is still one of the most popular stories told in Mizoram, where 98 percent of the population has been Christianized. One discovers why this is so when traveling through that state, particularly in the south. On a superficial level, the Mizos, unlike any other Northeast Indian community, deny having anything to do with pre-Christian cults. Yet most houses in rural areas are adorned with animal skulls, monkey tails, buffalo horns, tiger jaws and pig skins, owing to their presumed apotropaic qualities. Still widely accepted is the belief that the souls of wild animals, such as the tiger, may take possession of a person. A similar Mizo belief is that anyone wandering about alone at dawn is in fact a dead body that has been possessed by an ancestor's soul.

It is therefore difficult to believe that the Mizos have embraced Christianity completely—at least their manner of practicing Christianity must differ considerably from the way it is practiced in the West. Moreover many of the new customs seem curiously pietistic, such as the exaggerated, almost Sabbath-like intensity with which the laws of Sunday are heeded: no one is allowed to do anything but go to church, three to four times every Sunday. Visiting a Christian service in Mizoram, Nagaland or Meghalaya reveals the extent to which the ancient tribal cults are still alive—but also the clever means employed be the missionaries to convert the indigenous peoples. Drums, for example, ancient symbols of tribal identity, are the main instruments played in a Northeast Indian Christian service. The songs are more magical in character than pious. It would seem that the tenacity with which the ancient cults persisted had forced missionaries to adapt their tactics accordingly. However this approach was taken in view of the—dubious—success of initial missionary activities in the mid-19th century. Christianizing at that time was an almost militant affair, which involved the strict condemnation and banning of all ancient traditions, especially those associated with fertility cults. While promising a higher standard of living (for which the missionaries built schools), evoking hope of paradise and instilling fear of burning in hell if the ancient cults were not abandoned, American Baptist missionaries destroyed the woodcarvings of the Naga *morungs* and prohibited the performance of ancient songs and dances, the custom of sleeping in bachelors'

usually believed to embody. As a Sangtam-Naga explains: "My soul does not live in my body. It is not in me now. It lives in the leopard. It visits me in my sleep. I meet it in my dreams. Then I know what it has been doing. If anything were to happen to my leopard during the day, my soul would come and tell me. The next day I would have the same wounds as the leopard." Similar notions are extended to include tigers and mithans.[10] To this day the Garos of Meghalaya carry on the unique spiritual tradition of *jadoreng*—the ability of certain people psychologically and, to a certain extent, physically to turn into a tiger! The

tiger is regarded as the "wise brother," the alter ego, man's totem—recalling the shamanistic practices of native South Americans, who are purported to roam the forests as panthers in a similar state. The physical aspect of this may be inferred from reports in which shamans are said to act like tigers (by growling or stalking prey, for example) and even to smell intensely like tigers whenever they fall into this trance. According to reliable sources, an increased number of tigers in the surrounding jungles during these sessions has also been reported.[11]

Despite the animistic concept of nature clearly revealed in the Mizo story of the

Left: *The Great Indian Hornbill is the most revered bird in the indigenous societies of Northeast India. Mogh people with their prey.*
Photograph: C. D. Brauns.

Above: *A Thadou-Kuki woman wearing headgear displaying locusts' shells, which is worn during the hornbill dance.* Right: *Kabui-Nagas in their wedding attire. The man's headdress represents the hornbill.*
Photographs: P. Nalin.

dormitories, drinking rice beer and giving feasts of merit. The converted were taught to despise the "heathens," which frequently caused the break up of villages, leading to new ones being founded elsewhere. However, the fragmentation among the Nagas was not always as obvious as this. The new religion alone was often enough to break down the strong communal ties that had existed. Christianized Nagas suddenly found themselves released from their former duties, such as assisting with the harvest, if they fell on a Sunday. Furthermore they were given to believe that it had become unnecessary to participate in such communal activities as harvesting rice for a village festival or pitching in to prepare presents for an important guest. Ancient blood ties were no longer important. Quarrels about religion ensued, breaking up entire families. Christianized individuals began to wear Western clothes, abandoning the symbolic and

prestigious adornments they had once donned—the final nail in the coffin of ancient Naga culture.

That the missionaries replaced traditional values with education was disliked by the British colonial rulers. Their policy was to forbid such traditions as head-hunting, but to leave the rest of Naga culture untouched. By sealing off the Naga Hills from the rest of India and by shielding its peoples from any outside influences, the British intended to keep them ignorant in order to prevent uprisings occurring in yet another region of an already insurgent India.[12] In Mizoram the politically highly influential Catholic Church, with its pietistic policies, such as banning alcohol and contraceptives, is on its way to causing a rebellion among the young people, who are particularly susceptible to the material aspects of Western culture. The Church's outdated views, which fail sufficiently to take into account Mizoram's cultural heritage, have led to a renewed interest in traditional customs, notably among the upper classes and young people. In Arunachal Pradesh all Christian missionaries have been banned from the state by government decree—the result of a development that was initiated years ago by activist groups, such as "Kine-Name-Doibote" ("Earth-Mother-Sky"). Founded by the Pangi-Adis, this movement spread across the state, encouraging people to revert to their belief in "Mother Earth" and "Father Heaven."[13] Nagaland harbors similar groups, such as the Heraka cult and the Zeliangrong movement. The first was founded in 1925 by Jadonang, a Naga shaman and his cousin Gaidinliu. The cult combines many ancient Naga beliefs with the concept of monotheism. The founders sought to preserve the cultural identity of the Nagas, to examine critically the content of their religious concepts and to reform them if necessary. At the same time they endeavored to provide the people with the advantages introduced by the missionaries, such as health care, education and a higher standard of living, no matter what religion one professed.[14] Today, after many years of social unrest and internal fighting in Nagaland—initially between the Nagas and the Indian army, later among the Nagas themselves—the Church has turned to encouraging the revival of the traditional

Naga culture. After banning and systematically destroying it for nearly 150 years, the Church now takes the stance that reviving these traditions, a complex system of values that could instill in people a sense of national identity, may bring peace once again to Nagaland and Manipur.

It would seem that only the Khasis of Meghalaya have been able to integrate Christianity into their lives without radically changing their society or destroying their cultural identity. The matrilineal system has been preserved as well as the severe clan laws relating to exogamy and inheritance, and the belief in the connection between illness and spirits. A kind of syncretism has taken place, but it remains uncertain whether the absolutism that has marked Christianity throughout its long history will eventually make itself felt or whether the many religions practiced in this region will continue to coexist peacefully.[15]

In conclusion it may be said that most of the Northeast Indian peoples have a rather unorthodox attitude toward the world religions, despite the fact that they have been exposed to them for centuries. This applies to Christianity as well as Hinduism and Buddhism. For example, in a temple of the Assamese Deori people, who have converted to Hinduism, one finds not a single image of a deity—which is highly unusual among practitioners of the popular

form of Hinduism, with its vast pantheon. Moreover the churches of the Christianized Lisu, a small community in eastern Arunachal Pradesh, are utterly devoid of religious imagery, be it a representation of Jesus or the cross.[16]

To this day none of the indigenous peoples has been dissuaded from venerating spirits, which they continue to believe animate houses and nature, regardless of how deeply devoted they are to a world religion. Indeed animism is firmly rooted in the mentality of Northeast Indians.

Bottom left: *Pride and fearlessness mark the eyes of these two Konyak-Naga children.* Photograph: P. Nalin.

Bottom right: *This old Wancho man from the village of Dadam reveals the unorthodox attitude of the tribal population toward Christianity: his chest is traditionally tattooed, mountain goat horns adorn his ears and tiger claws decorate his chest, as does the rather incongruous Christian cross.* Photograph: G. Horter.

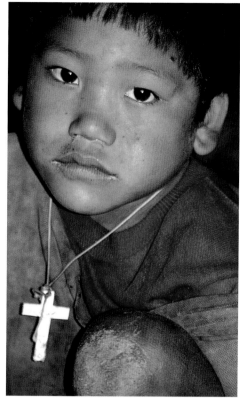

"LOSS OF RELIGION IS LOSS OF CULTURE
LOSS OF CULTURE IS LOSS OF IDENTITY"

ALL-IN-CHURCH FELLOWSHIP

Top: *In war-torn Nagaland bamboo toy guns have replaced carved toys of animals.* Bottom: *Certain aspects of Hindu worship have been assimilated into Nocte culture. Behind a Shiva-lingam the trinity of Brahma, Vishnu and Shiva is depicted in traditional wooden sculptures.* Photograph: G. Horter.

Above and right: *Christian missionaries have left their mark on Northeast India as have the turbulent times that emerged in the wake of their activities here.*

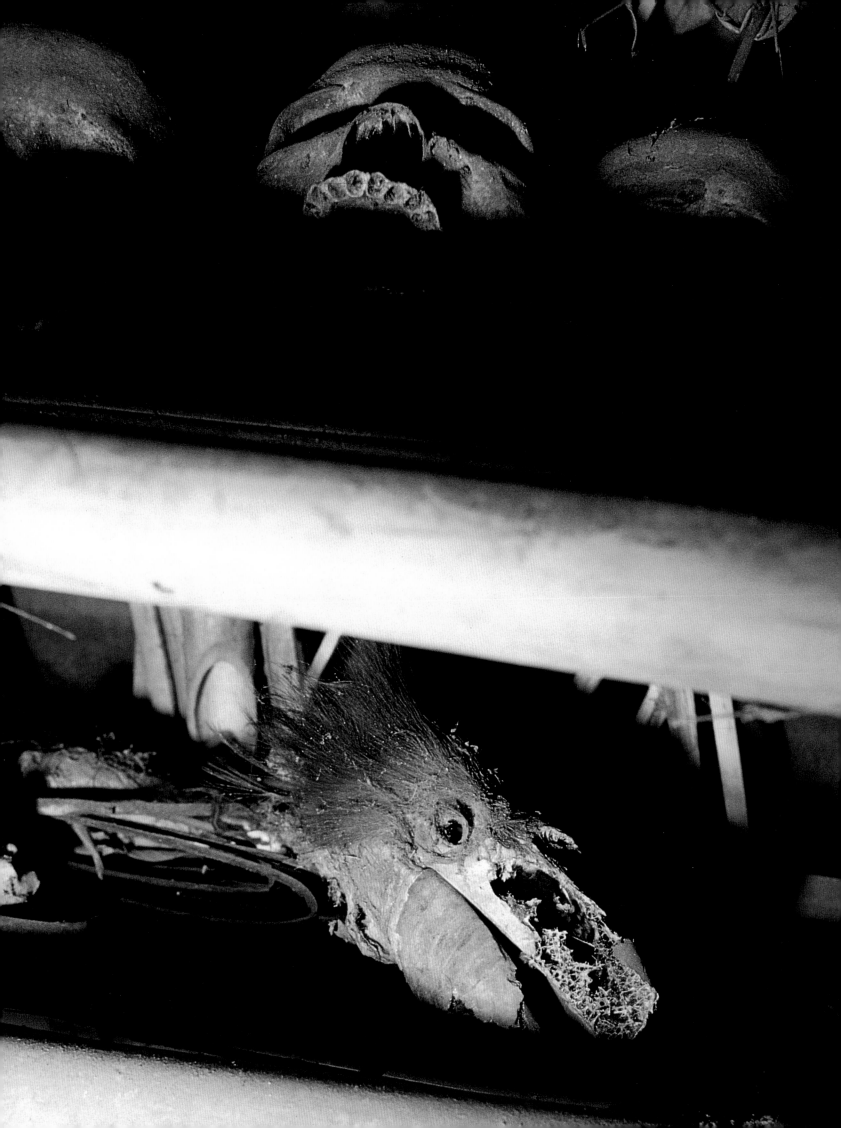

12

FERTILITY THROUGH STONES AND HEADS

POWER THROUGH PAIN

Tsungrangre, you are our village god.
May we have bountiful harvests!
Therefore bestow upon us many heads!
(Sangtam-Naga prayer uttered before felling
a tree that is to become the new log drum)[1]

The deeply spiritual aspect of the sacrificial cults of Northeast India finds expression in other customs of the region's inhabitants as well. Over the years the Khasis in Meghalaya, the Mizos and the Nagas, for example, have erected stone monuments, which has led to the emergence of a megalith culture rich in symbolism.

Megaliths, here composed of three, five or seven crudely carved stones of varying sizes, are encountered throughout the Khasi Hills. These monuments bear witness to the tradition of ancestor worship so central to *Niam Khasi*, the religion of the Khasis. Several types of stone monument are erected in memory of deceased relatives. *Mawbynnas* generally consist of several one- to five-m-high menhirs surrounding a larger central monolith, referred to as the "uncle stone," and are dedicated to the *kni*, the maternal uncle of the youngest girl in the family of the deceased. The outer stones represent the male ancestors of the family, whereas the monolith at the center is the petrified clan mother and primal mother in

Human skulls and a hornbill beak displayed at the
morung of the Nocte village of Lapnan.

one and is used as an altar during burial ceremonies. Thus the group of stones symbolizes the entire clan and serves to pay tribute to the ancestors of the Khasis, both real and mythological. In ancient times a male member of the community was sacrificed every year to the ancestress in order to ensure the clan's survival and continued well-being; later food was placed before the stones as offerings instead.

The second type is called the *mawnam* and is arranged in a similar fashion, but is dedicated to the family of the deceased's father. Stone megaliths are also found along paths leading to clan graves and usually consist of three one-m-high boulders with a flat stone placed in front of them. These *mawlyntis* are intended to serve as resting places for the maternal family's spirits on their way to the clan grave. Another type is called the "stone of oath," which is used to resolve disputes. Since it is believed that the stone embodies the spirit of an ancestor, an oath pledged in its presence is a sacred act. Breaking it is tantamount to committing a mortal sin.

Since stone burials play such an integral part in the religious life of the Khasis, the religion could be characterized as a "funerary religion." Traditional Khasi burial rites can be broken down into three distinct stages. First the deceased is cremated. The ashes and remaining bones are then collected by the youngest daughter, who, years later, will bury them beneath the dolmen in front of the clan grave. Thus is

the deceased's soul thought to be able to rejoin the primal mother. Later an additional stone is erected in the clan grave to commemorate the dead relative. Clan graves therefore usually cover extremely large areas, which presumably was thought to conciliate the dead and prevent them from returning as ghosts. Only fifty years ago the Khasis were still known to carry giant boulders to burial sites, which were often some considerable distance from where the boulders were found. They were transported merely by means of ropes and wooden cylinders. At the grave, pits were dug, into which the boulders were lowered. With the exception of erecting a new monolith for every relative who passes away, the Khasi funerary tradition remains alive today, despite strong Christian influences.[2]

Mizoram also boasts numerous monuments that were raised to commemorate the dead. It was once common among the various Mizo peoples of this state to immortalize a dead clan chief by erecting wooden or stone posts at his grave. These posts were incised with stylized portraits of the deceased, his family and his worldly possessions. Moreover his hunting trophies were also depicted, which often included tigers, elephants, hornbills, wild boars and mithans either hunted or sacrificed by him at feasts of merit (see below), as well as enemies killed and slaves caught by him. Chiefs were therefore frequently portrayed holding the head of one of their victims in one hand and a

weapon in the other (apparently a reminder of the cultural affinity between the early Mizos and the Nagas), surrounded by animals.[3] Since one post was not sufficient to depict all the feasts of merit given by the deceased, it was not uncommon to erect several additional monuments above the burial site. An extraordinary example of such a monument is located on the present-day school grounds in the village of Ruantlang in Mizoram's Champhai District, near the Burman border. Among a group of five boulders, all of which bear carvings—such as a human figure with outstretched arms, surrounded by mithan skulls—one is particularly noteworthy: its front shows four rows of twenty-four figures above six mithan skulls. The top of the boulder has been broken off and is on display in the small museum of Champhai town.

A cursory glance at the boulder might lead one to conclude that it commemorates a clan chief. However, the locals call this stone the *Chhura fa rep*, denoting "memorial stone in honor of Chhura," Mizoram's mythical national hero. Local opinion would seem to vary on Chhura's merit. Some think he was simply a fool; others believe that profound wisdom and selfless love for his brother, Nahaia, caused him to act as he did. The episode in Chhura's life probably depicted on the stone goes something like this:

Chhura and Nahaia each had their own field. On Nahaia's field stood a hollow tree, which was inhabited by a tree spirit and her babies. The cowardly and shrewd Nahaia convinced Chhura to swap fields with him, without explaining why. After the matter had been settled, Nahaia told Chhura that if he threw a stone at the big tree, many pigeons would come out, which he could kill for meat. When the latter threw a stone, the spirit fled from the tree, leaving her babies behind. Chhura killed them all and took them home to eat.[4]

The twenty-four figures could represent the tree spirit's babies. The tip of the boulder shows Chhura holding a typical dagger of a Mizo hunter. The stone megalith culture is still alive in Mizoram, although it now draws on a Christian tradition, for today such stone memorials bear merely the birth and death dates of the deceased.

Curiously enough in Tripura the

Top left: *The Chhura stone at Ruantlang, Mizoram.* Center and bottom left: *Khasi megaliths near the villages of Smit and Nartiang, where a veritable "monolith park" is located in a sacred grove.* Below: *Fragment of an ancient burial stone from Mizoram. It depicts the deeds of the deceased, who can be seen in the lower left. He is shown holding a head-hunter's spear in one hand and his pipe in the other and is surrounded by the animals he hunted in his lifetime.*

Chakmas use stones during purification ceremonies in which the *ojha*, or village priest, crushes small pebbles in a mortar and murmurs: "I shall create a sea by crushing these stones. I shall turn all habitations into a watery surface. I shall draw water from the running brook. I shall purify the inane human beings and send them to their houses. O mother, please hear my prayers."[5] Once a year hundreds of pilgrims flock to a magnificent stone monument, called Unakoti, near the village of Kailashahar in northern Tripura. The hilly enclave, whose name signifies "a million minus one," is presently in danger of being reclaimed by the jungle. Covering a stone wall measuring one square kilometer in size are hundreds of stone reliefs bearing depictions of human figures, heads and animals. Numerous sandstone sculptures, temple ruins and footpaths are to be found scattered along a brook.

Various myths are associated with the site. One recounts that an inspired artist had planned to carve a million figures in a single day to pay homage to the gods. But when the sun rose the following day he had completed all but one carving. Overcome with vexation, the sculptor threw himself off a cliff. According to Hindu legend a million gods are said to have met at Unakoti one night to undertake a pilgrimage to the sacred town of Benares. However one of the gods was missing. Although Shiva urged the others to proceed with their journey, they refused to start without their friend. Thus it so happened that they all turned to stone the following morning at the first cry of the crow.

Archaeologists date the Unakoti complex between the 11th and the 15th century. Stylistically the carvings are like no others encountered in Indian art. Instead they bear an astonishing resemblance to the art associated with the *devaraja* cult practiced by the Khmers of Cambodia, which may have found its way to Tripura via the Arakan Hills, northern Burma, Manipur, Ahom or Cachar. It seems likely that local artists of the Tibetan Burmese people made the carvings. The large *dheri* earrings that are depicted, which are unknown in Indian art but are worn by some of the indigenous peoples of Tripura, would seem to support this hypothesis. The faces are portrayed with eyes that are slightly almond shaped (perhaps reflecting the shape of the artist's own eyes), practically no eyebrows and mouths largely consisting of narrow slits

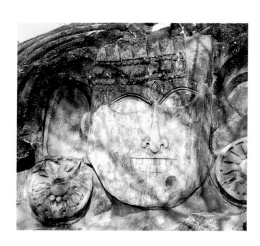

Rock carvings at Unakoti, Tripura. Top left: A bowl bearing head reliefs. Left center: A depiction of the sun god. Bottom left: A composite being. Top right: A deity's face on the central rock. Bottom right: A hunter and a deity.

with simple vertical lines as teeth.[6] Their facial expressions would seem to indicate that the figures are in a state of wrath rather than spiritual enlightenment.

Interpreting the Unakoti carvings raises several problems: if it is true that the motifs have been drawn from Hindu mythology and that the male figures represent such Hindu gods as Shiva and Vishnu, they are yet another instance of the indigenous inhabitants' unorthodox attitude toward the world religions. The deities in particular, which are dated to another period on stylistic grounds, would appear to be products of a magical, demonic worldview, marked by the belief in spirits, nature worship, hunting and clan feuds—all aspects that are far removed from the lofty, spiritual and highly symbolic concepts of Hinduism. Moreover this is also reflected in the human figures, which are shown carrying bows and arrows, and whose head-gear recalls that of the Nagas and peoples of Arunachal Pradesh. Depictions of composite beings, composed of animal bodies and human heads, which reveal the widespread belief in the transmigration of human souls into animals, would also suggest that the artist had an animistic worldview, as well as the fact that mostly heads are depicted. Does this perhaps speak in favor of a connection to the head-hunting tradition of Northeast India?

The most interesting stone cults were once found among the Nagas. One custom involved erecting a stone megalith every time a man had premarital sex, earning him social prestige as such practices were thought to attest to his virility, thus fertility, which plays such a central role in the religious life of the Nagas.

Another reason for erecting such monuments was to mark the occasion of feasts of merit, which were celebrated in stages. First taboos were observed: certain food and drink had to be abstained from, certain clothes worn and new rites performed involving adorning one's house with, for example, mithan horns, phallic symbols and *morung* carvings. Every stage was more exacting of the host than the previous one in that the number of mithans sacrificed and the quantity of rice beer increased at each. Only once the final stage of the feast was completed was a megalith erected, the stones of which symbolized the wealth of the host. By giving feasts of merit the host was elevated in status and ensured that he would not be forgotten after death.[7]

Stone monuments of the Maram-, Mao- and Konyak-Nagas. Top: Stones symbolizing female fertility, erected in a Mao village. Center: Monoliths in the blood red soil of a field near the village of Intu, symbolizing the power of fertility. Bottom: Dolmans in front of two Maram houses.
Right: A Maram-Naga woman returns home after a hard day in the fields. Her path near the village of Purul Atongba winds through an assemblage of stone errections that have been posted here in order to achieve the soil's fertility.
Photographs: P. Nalin.

Several villages in Arunachal Pradesh's Tirap District and in Nagaland, particularly those inhabited by chiefs, still have bachelors' dormitories containing log drums. These instruments, made from hollowed-out trees trunks, which today are played at festivals only, used to be played prior to head-hunts. In only a few remaining morungs, do human skulls taken from former raids still hang on the walls.

Female and male fertility was often associated with erecting stones, which had the same symbolic significance as the often Y-shaped fertility posts. The "Y" symbolized the female sex, whereas a simple pole represented a phallus. This symbolic dimension explains the real meaning of the feasts of merit: a host who was able to reach the final stage, owing to his material wealth, acquired the reputation of being a "carrier of great fertility" and his elevated status was recognized officially. The final stage was intended to transfer the personal merit of the feast giver to the entire community. In it all the men in the village erected an enormous stone or lowered a new fertility post into the earth, both symbolic gestures of the host's fertility sinking back into the soil.[8] Giving such feasts was so costly that, as in Apa Tani society, the host's material wealth was reduced to the level of the rest of the villagers, which served to reintegrate him into society. That such feasts were held during harvest and sowing celebrations reveals yet another aspect thereof: that, for the Nagas, fertility, human sexuality and bountiful harvests were interrelated and could be favorably influenced by human beings. Since holding feasts of merit was contingent upon whether one had sufficient means to do so, that is, that one owned the necessary number of productive fields, this custom encouraged agricultural competition among villagers. Additionally the feasts also provided the ideal opportunity to use up perishable goods and crops. The leveling effect and the reintegration of the host into society provided a welcome relief from the often severely autocratic social structures of the clans, which attributed absolute power to a single chief or a group of village elders. By returning the material wealth to the community, the communal balance was redressed.[9]

The fertility cult, an integral aspect of religious thought among most Northeast Indian peoples, also found expression in other, more gruesome traditions, such as head-hunting, which was at one time widespread in Northeast India. In order to understand this custom, which today is deemed as barbaric, one must realize that symbolically laden, metaphysical concepts underlay it. Its complexity, much like the philosophical underpinnings of the gruesome human sacrifices performed by the Mayas in Central America, may certainly be

regarded as a cultural achievement. Reduced to a simple formula the concept underlying the custom is: heads are equated with fertility.

One people that practised head-hunting were the Nagas. Like most peoples of the world, the Nagas believe that the human soul is located in the head. They even believe that they can offer "proof" of this, for they ascribe the shifting of an infant's fontanel after birth to the soul (*tenela*) inside. For the Chang-Nagas yawning is thought to be caused by an impatient soul dancing around in the mouth while waiting to leave the body once asleep.[10] As was discussed in the previous chapter, the Nagas believe that human beings have several souls, one of which remains inside the head after death and is a source of fertile potency, which can be transmitted to others. Thus the only means of acquiring such power was to behead one's enemies.

When the village leaders, that is the chief, the shaman or the elders, agreed that a head-hunt had become necessary—either to ensure fecundity in the fields, to reinvigorate a village community or to inaugurate a magical institution, such as a new log drum—the performance of a three-part ritual was begun after the oracle had been consulted by the shaman. First the village had to undergo a ritual during which sacrifices were made at the fertility stones and taboos were observed in order to strengthen the hostile forces within the head-hunters and to remove them spiritually from everyday experience. In this volatile and hostile state an enemy village would be attacked.

Head-hunting peoples sometimes distinguished between the heads of men, women and children. The Sema-Nagas, for example, valued women's heads more highly than men's, for women were believed to possess the greatest fertility potency. The Thadou-Kukis placed the highest value on the heads of children, whether male or female, since capturing them would require the warrior to enter the enemy's village (however, the Lhota-Nagas never took the heads of children whose teeth had not been filed down). The second most highly prized heads of the Thadou-Kukis were those of women, for the hunter would have to get very close to the enemy's village to capture them. Then came the heads of enemy warriors, since it would require great skill and strength to kill them. Heads were hung from the village "head tree," either a ficus or a cactuslike euphorbia, both of which exude a milky substance when pierced, which is thought to symbolize the essence of the soul contained in the victim's head. Offerings were then made to the head. In order to appease the spirit and to encourage it to call on its relatives, so that they too could be killed, many Naga peoples fed the "soul in the head" of the enemy by placing morsels of food in the mouth and eyes, inducing it to call on the souls of its relatives and lure them into a trap by promising them a similar feast. Thus the wives of the Ao-Naga warriors fed the heads while uttering the words: "I am feeding you. Bring your father, your mother and your sons and daughters."

Having returned from a successful head-hunt, the warriors would be regarded as sacrosanct, yet also as impure and dangerously unpredictable. In huts specially built for them, they were forced to undergo another period of sexual abstinence, to wear all-white garments and to eat a special diet, prepared exclusively by men. Only by means of a final purification ritual involving both the head-hunters and the captured heads were the warriors reintegrated into society. The entire village would dance

around the head, or heads, to the beat of large drums, ritual songs were sung and a feast of merit was held. Adolescents were allowed to touch the heads with their *daos*, thus inducting them into the head-hunting tradition. After the celebrations were over the heads were

only rarely kept in private homes, for the Nagas feared their victims' souls. For this reason, Ao-Nagas always hung a dog's skull above that of their enemy, believing that if the dead man's relatives called on him in dreams to tell them who had taken his life, the dog's barking would drown out his voice, thus preventing an answer being communicated. The Yacham- and Konyak-Nagas' custom of fixing water buffalo horns to the ears of a head served two purposes: to associate the victim with the fruits of the earth and to render it deaf.

The heads were usually displayed in the most fertile place in the village: inside the *morung*, the chief's house, the house of the log drum at the fertility pole or at stone monuments, where they were frequently buried so that the fertility they possessed could be transmitted to all the head-hunters who participated in the raid and would be returned to the earth. A successful head-

A head-hunting ceremony performed by Konyak-Nagas from the village of Aopao. The warriors have put themselves into a hostile mood by chewing hot chilies and other spicy food and by dancing for hours on end. The human head has been replaced by a beet attached to a pole erected on enemy territory. The warriors dance around it until, eventually, a designated dancer—usually a man who is about to marry and therefore must perform his "manly" duties—will cut the pole and beat down with his dao. Photographs: P. Nalin.

Top left: Tegwos, or "precious stones," at a chief's house in the Wancho village of Nginu, Arunachal Pradesh. These stones are believed to possess fertility power and are closely associated with head-hunting. Top right: Fertility ceremonies have been performed at this stone in the village of Maram Khullen, northern Manipur, which is indicated by the bamboo fence surrounding the site. Photograph: P. Nalin. Bottom left: A phallic stone erected in the village of Maram Khullen. Engraved on one side is the number of feasts of merit given by the man who had it erected.

Bottom right: These buffalo skulls hanging from a former "head tree" in the village of Nginu have replaced human skulls, which used to be displayed here after successful head-hunts. Opposite: This carved wooden head has been placed on freshly ground grain, Maram, northern Manipur. It symbolizes a human skull, which in former times would have been used to direct the person's fertility onto the food.

hunt was regarded as definitive proof that head-hunters were in direct contact with fertility powers. By capturing a head, a hunter was thought to become part of these forces, was animated by them, as were the other members of the community.

Head-hunting was regarded as a form of transmutation. By killing another person, a warrior transformed life into death. The accompanying rituals transformed the biological fact of death into social or cultural values, whose symbol was the head. However, it was not always deemed necessary to take heads to accomplish the aims of head-hunting. The same cult status could be achieved by capturing the heads of tigers, leopards, monkeys and the mithans of one's enemies, as well as other parts of the human body, such as hands, feet and ears. Often it was deemed sufficient for a warrior to pierce with his dagger the corpse of the enemy whose head had been cut off to acquire the same prestige as the head-hunter himself.[11]

A high value was also given to heads from one's own village. However the customs surrounding them embrace the Nagas' belief in the existence of a soul, which does not necessarily relate to the fertility cult. The Khiamniungam-Nagas used to dry corpses by smoking them, place them in canoelike coffins and hang them from the eaves of the dead person's house. In the interim little huts on stilts were erected, completely furnished in miniature form for the souls of the dead to inhabit. On the first day of the taboo period connected with the new year's sowing period all the bodies of people who had died the previous year were taken out of their coffins, the bones were removed and put into phallic-shaped vessels, which were stored in the family's granary. The remains of the flesh and wrappings were returned to the coffin, which was then pushed off a cliff. When crops were harvested, a small portion was placed in the miniature house, which served as provisions for the deceased on their journey to *timpu*, the land of the dead. Thereafter the miniature house was forgotten, as was the deceased.[12] This cultic process reveals the Naga belief that human death and agricultural "birth" are linked. The dead person's fertility power is believed to be released when his bones are deposited in the urn, which was done before seeds were sown in the fields. It was assumed that this power would be transmitted to the earth's soil and fertilize the crops, just as the contents of the granary were thought to be favorably affected by the vessel placed therein. Nevertheless the soul was believed to inhabit the miniature house, attesting to the Naga belief that human beings have several souls. The same notion is revealed in the funerary cults of the Konyak-Nagas and the Wanchos, who still behead their dead, place the heads in earthen vessels and feed them. They believe that one soul leaves the body at death, whereas a second one roams the house aimlessly. It can reach the realm of the dead only once its head has been cut

off, taken into the house, washed, fed and placed in a receptacle. Similar customs are known among the Tripuris, who, shortly after cremating their dead, remove a piece of the skull and place it with incense and candles on a miniature boat made from leaves, which is thought to be navigated by two dolls that function as rowers to the realm of the dead, and set the boat out on the river.[13]

The Nagas believed that, even long after the death of a great head-hunter or feast giver, the community could benefit from his fertility power time and again. Wooden figures of deceased notables were therefore carved in times of "low levels of fertility." These figures were placed on their respective graves and along paths leading to the fields or inside granaries, which was thought to make the earth fecund once again. Yet, in some Naga societies, these

carvings served merely to commemorate deceased persons. Other groups combined both concepts by fixing the skull of the dead person to the carved figure, which was thought to make the fertility stored inside the head return to the soil via the wooden "conductor."[14]

Much importance was attached to the public display of one's elevated social status acquired through head-hunting or feast giving. Hunters were awarded adornments symbolizing their new status either by the village chief himself or by middlemen. These decorations varied from people to people, but they all represented variations on the same theme: "fertility," a message that was always intelligible to the other members of the community. They often came in the form of cowry shells; bone bracelets decorated with dyed goat hair; necklaces; and pearl, brass or boar-tusk bangles,

whose number indicated the number of heads captured during a raid. Special fabrics, shawls and blankets were also reserved for hunters and feast givers.[15] The Wanchos living in the border region of Arunachal Pradesh and Nagaland decorated articles of everyday life with fertility symbols, such as tobacco pipes, combs and hair pins. Each people employed its own ornaments, which served to convey messages to other members of the community. Men in particular made frequent use of them to display their status as head-hunters. Since head-hunting is no longer practiced among the Nagas, the symbols associated with this tradition are rapidly falling out of use or being replaced by other practices, such as holding feasts of merit.[16] It still generally holds true that the traditional clothes, headgear and adornments worn by the peoples, especially of Arunachal Pradesh and Tripura, serve to distinguish their wearers.

Another tradition in this regard that is still alive among several Northeast Indian peoples is tattooing. The purpose of this painful custom is twofold: to distinguish individuals inside and outside a given community. In such societies tattoos are compulsory, for they facilitate the identification of a fellow tribesman in war, for example, while also indicating the rank and status of individuals within a society. Apa Tani and Aka women of Arunachal Pradesh and Karbi women of Assam tattoo their faces, which identifies them as belonging to their respective tribes. Since they are applied to mark certain rites of passage (such as entering adulthood, becoming a mother, etc.), they indicate the person's social status to other members of the community. The same applies to Wancho women: when they are betrothed at six or seven years of age, three lines are tattooed along the navel. The first menstruation is marked by zigzag lines along the calves, symbolizing the formal act of betrothal. Before women leave their parental home to live with their husbands, vertical lines are tattooed above the knee and horizontal lines below it. An M-shaped tattoo is added to the women's chests either during their seventh month of pregnancy or right after having had their first child. Contrary to Wancho men, it is forbidden to tattoo the faces of women.[17] Among the Wanchos and the Konyak-Nagas tattoos likewise serve to document men's "fertility status" and their contact with female cosmological forces. In former times these attributes were

associated with head-hunting, however, since this tradition has been banned, it has been replaced with giving feasts of merit or has been transformed into altered or merely symbolic forms of head-hunting. If a Wancho youth wishes to marry, he still must first take part in a symbolic head-hunting raid. His friends hide a wooden figure in a former enemy's territory. The young warrior leads his friends on the hunt, finds and "kills" the wooden enemy, whereupon he brings the figure's head home as a trophy. Sometimes it is regarded as sufficient to bring home a tuft of grass or some bushes found growing in an enemy's field—the grass presumably symbolizing the enemy's hair. To this day in some remote villages of Arunachal Pradesh's Tirap District and Naga-land's Mon District participating in mock head-hunts is the only way for a bachelor to earn the right to be tattooed, without which it would not be possible for him to marry or pass on his fertility.[18]

Tattooing is an extremely arduous process, demanding great patience and physical endurance of the person being tattooed, for the "operations" are extremely painful. By consulting the oracles the shaman fixes the date of the tattooing session, which is followed by a feast that is held for the entire village. Inside the *morung* an expert (usually a woman, such as the chief's wife, who may be paid only in kind for her services) first applies with black soot the patterns suitable for the person's status to the appropriate parts of the body, such as the face, throat, chest or back. Then the patterns are tapped into the skin with a needle made from a thorn. An assistant keeps the skin taut. After this has been completed, the patterns are lubricated with a blue mixture made from the sap of a plant. This is excruciating and usually causes the skin to become inflamed, in extreme cases to the point that the person is unable to move for days or even weeks on end.[19] Owing to the extreme physical pain caused by the tattooing process, the Nagas regard a tattoo as a sign of strength, courage and virility. In addition to covering the person's body, the tattoo lends him an aura of dangerousness. Moreover tattoos applied to the face, much like war paint, give the person a fierce, mask-like expression, which, together with the knowledge of how such tattoos are earned, namely by demonstrat-ing one's head-hunting prowess, enhances this impression even further.

Opposite, left column. From top to bottom: *A display of skulls in the administrative section of the Thangkul-Naga township of Ukhrul.* Photograph: H. Sanghvi. *Enemies' heads at Lapnan. Part of the skull collection of the Wancho villages of Wakka and Konnu.* Lower two photographs: G. Horter. Opposite, right, from top to bottom: *Ancient carvings of heads on the gate of a Thangkul-Naga house. The intricately carved facade of a posingka, or a head-hunter's house, in the Maram village of Oinam, Manipur, showing human and buffalo heads as well as upside down tigers and human figures.* Photographs: P. Nalin.

Chief's house in a Maram village. The top row displays carvings of members of the chief's family, stylized human heads, stools and hornbill beaks. The rest of the entrance is adorned with alternating buffalo heads and carvings of human heads (detail). Above: *Skulls prominently displayed inside a Konyak-Naga morung. They have been fixed to water buffalo horns in order to associate the victims with the fruits of the earth and to render their souls deaf.* Photograph: H. Sanghvi.

In Naga societies skilled head-hunters and feast givers were and still are entitled to adorn their houses with the symbols of their status. Very few of these houses, which attest to the great skill of local craftsmen, have survived the influence of Christianization. Left: Carvings in the chief's house in the village of Pudunamei, Senapati District, northern Manipur, representing members of his family. Top: The outer and inner walls of a head-hunter's house in Maram are adorned with highly symbolic carvings. The walls of the ritual room bear depictions of human figures whose heads appear between the legs of other figures and whose penises are clearly visible, symbolizing the life-engendering power of head-hunting. Spears have been placed next to the entrance, signifying that no one is allowed in this room except the shaman and the owner. Bottom: The entrance walls of two Maram-Naga chief's houses, bearing depictions of human figures and heads in relief, as well as mithan heads and hornbill beaks.
Right photograph: P. Nalin.

A unique piece of woodcarving is displayed in the chief's house of the Konyak-Naga village of Shangnyu. Entering the house through a door next to a carving of a stylized elephant one encounters a fertility shrine worked out of a single piece of wood. It is about 20 feet long and 12 feet high and originally was about 6 ft. thick. The thickness was cut away, leaving all sorts of carvings, some in high relief, other parts standing on projecting ledges and cut entirely away from the background, but all done in the same piece of wood. The carvings are: two tigers, one damaged, the other realistically depicted, above a row of human heads, borne by two naturalistically rendered hoolock gibbons.

Several warriors are adorned with mithan horns and feathers and hold daos and heads in their hands. Tattoos are painted on the surface, and their penises are shown erect. Additional carvings include a mother suckling her child (damaged); a man and a woman having sexual intercourse; a cock crowing; a large snake; a double rainbow and a basket that is separate from the main scene, hollowed out on the inside to be used as a receptacle with a removable cover. Four more standing figures have been attached to the shrine since Verrier Elwin last documented the site in the 1950s.
Photographs: P. Nalin

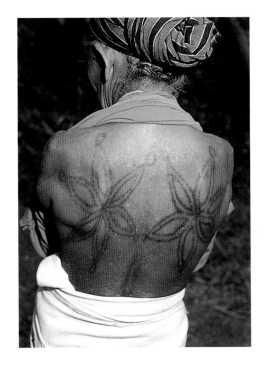

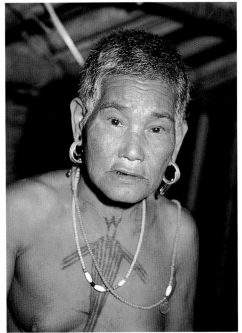

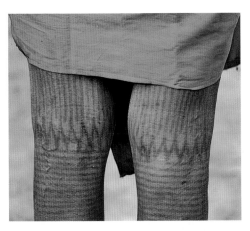

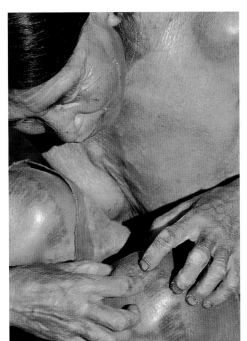

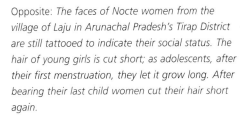

Opposite: *The faces of Nocte women from the village of Laju in Arunachal Pradesh's Tirap District are still tattooed to indicate their social status. The hair of young girls is cut short; as adolescents, after their first menstruation, they let it grow long. After bearing their last child women cut their hair short again.*

Top left: *Flower tattoos on the shoulder blades of a Nocte woman from the village of Kheti.* Center left: *Tattoos on the back of a Wancho woman's knees and legs. Photograph: A. Nath.* Bottom left: *Circular patterns tatooed on the shoulders and chest of a Nocte woman from Laho. Photograph: G. Horter,* Top and bottom center: *Tattoos of Wancho women, representing a human figure on the chest (Nginu, Tirap, Arunachal Pradesh) and on the knees (Pongchau).* Top and bottom right: *Facial tattoos of an Aka woman from Bhalukpong, West Kameng, Arunachal Pradesh and of a married Nocte woman from Laju.*

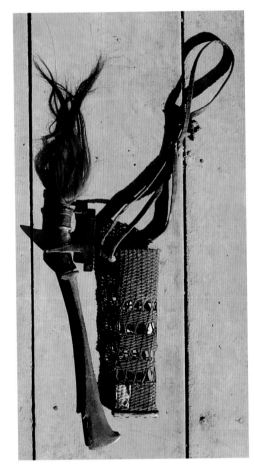

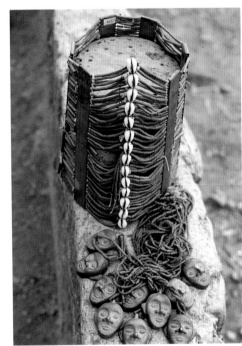

Top left: *Original carved wooden pendants worn by Wancho head-hunters in former times.* Bottom left: *A head-hunter's* dao *from Mizoram.* Top center, right and opposite: *Konyak Naga head-hunters.* Photographs: P. Nalin. Bottom center: *Original adornment made from brass with beads and cowry shells worn by Mizo head-hunters around the upper thigh. The number of brass heads indicates the number of heads the wearer has captured.* Bottom right: *A Wancho head-hunter adorned with chest and spectacle tatoos, wearing goat's horns through his earlobes.*

13

Women's Mysterious Realm

Imas, Matrilineality, and the Great Mother

A long time ago the Khasis living in the green hills of Meghalaya were not as numerous as they are today. Originally sixteen clans existed, from which all Khasis descend, and heaven and earth were united. Seven clans had seven huts on Mt. Sohpetbneng. The other nine clans had their own houses in heaven. A huge oak tree grew from the earth up into the clouds. At the center of the oak tree a ladder reached up into heaven. The clans visited each other via the ladder. Every visit was marked by a feast. The tree, which offered them its shade, grew bigger and mightier. One day a tiger approached the people of earth, treading softly. He spoke sweetly to them. He said they would benefit greatly by felling the tree. The people believed him and cut down the mighty oak tree. Then a great darkness enveloped the world. The sun vanished behind the dead tree and did not want to rise again. For many dark days the people looked for someone to help them. It was the cock who finally offered his services as a middleman. By crowing for many hours he finally managed to entice the sun to reappear. The heavenly ladder, however, had

The Molsum-Halams of Tripura venerate the forest goddess, Sengra, who brings fertility and prosperity to the people. Thus ecological balance is equated with prosperity.

disappeared and the connection to the huts in heaven had been severed. Ever since the people of the seven clans have tried to reestablish a link between heaven and earth, to no avail. Yet this ambition of the seven clans has led to their strength—the female strength of the Khasis, the origin of the people.[1]

In this Khasi myth women wield immense power, which derives from the separation of earth from paradise and from the efforts involved in attempting to reestablish this paradisiacal state. It does not, however, indicate the kinds of effort that are made in this respect. To gain more insight into this one must only look at how the inhabitants of Meghalaya, the "Abode of the Clouds," live together.

The societies of the Khasis, the Jaintias and the Garos are matrilineal, tracing descent through the maternal line—a social system that is otherwise very rare in the world today. This common principle unites them and serves as the central pillar around which their cultures have developed. Matrilineal descent forms the basis of these peoples' ethnic and religious identity. It is the root of their religion, which, among the Khasis, is an amalgamation of ethics, moral guidelines and codes of conduct, as laid down by their highest deities: U Blei Nongthaw, the Creator, and Ka Blei, Mother Nature, or the "mistress who rules over heaven and earth." As in Naga societies, the latter goddess is more important to the

Khasis since she affects their daily lives, as the name "mistress" suggests. That the principle governing earth is necessarily female derives from the Khasi belief that everything born on earth originates from a female body. This notion has a bearing on the way illegitimate children are viewed in Khasi society. Irrespective of whether they are born out of wedlock or not, all children are regarded as legitimate, for the Khasis have a saying: "Whereas motherhood is certain, fatherhood is nothing more than a myth."

Owing to the belief in a goddess ruling over the earth and the aforementioned Khasi creation myth, the clan mother is deemed the most important person in the community. As its chief and priestess, she administers the clan property as well as the income of the various family members. She is viewed as the worldly equivalent of the Primal Mother, Ka Blei. Evidence of the equally high status enjoyed by the Primal Mother and the clan mother can be found in the megalithic graves scattered across the Khasi Hills. The large stones resting in front of the gravestones are used as altars and graves for both—the Primal Mother and the clan mother (see previous chapter). Unlike in other Indian states, where female fetuses are frequently aborted, Khasi couples continue to have children until a daughter is born, for it is "only through daughters that the clan can be perpetuated." It is not the name of the man that is passed down, but that of the

woman. Children belong to the mother's maternal family, not to the father's. Descent is traced through the maternal line via the mother, the grandmother, the great grandmother, etc. Not only are worldly matters taken care of by women in Khasi society, but also the rituals surrounding ancestor worship. Since women are responsible for performing burials, it is also the women who "close the circle of life" by symbolically returning deceased clan members to the Primal Mother's womb by means of performing funeral rites at the clan grave.

Khasi funerals are deemed essential and, as a rule, are extremely costly. Traditional funeral rites are performed by the *khadduh*, the youngest daughter, even if she has been converted to Christianity, which is widespread in Maghalaya. Yet she may be expelled from her duties if, for example, she breaks one of the many taboos. She must observe the rules of exogamy, must not have been involved in the murder of a child, must not have been engaged in an incestuous affair, must not have remarried prematurely after a divorce, must be physically and mentally suitable for

the task, must not have been absent from the family for any great length of time and must assume the costs of the burial.

The various forms of marriage among the Khasis and the Garos also attest to the matrilineal character of their societies. Without this institution, which forms the very foundations of a family, communities would not be able to function.

The Duolocal Marriage

The most peculiar form of matrilineal marriage, which has survived in certain Jaintia villages, is the duolocal, or "visiting," marriage, whereby the husband is forbidden to enter the household of his wife and is not allowed to move into the house once their marriage has been consummated. He is and remains separate from his wife's family (*iing*) and clan (*kpho*). His visits merely serve the purpose of procreation, the perpetuation of his wife's clan. The man remains a member of his mother's and youngest sister's *iing*, tends his mother's and sister's fields and often sleeps in his maternal family's house. If he dies, he is interred in the clan grave of his maternal family. In this form of marriage the woman has the right to raise the children, run the household, administer the property, preserve the legacy of the ancestors and perform funeral rites. The husband in the duolocal marriage is merely the propagator of the clan: the only function and position for which he is respected. Rarely is he asked for his assistance or opinion, and women are the dominant figures in the family.

The Matrilocal and Uxorilocal Marriage

When a *khadduh* enters matrilocal marriage, her husband lives in the house of her mother. Together with the unmarried, divorced or widowed sons and daughters, uncles and aunts, they form a *kpoh*. If an elder daughter marries, the marriage is uxorilocal, whereby the couple moves into a dwelling attached to the house of the bride's mother, essentially cohabiting with the *iing khadduh*, the family of the youngest daughter. If more than one daughter in the family marries, their houses are grouped around the main house of their mother, transforming an *iing* into a *kpoh*. In this case the husband is entitled to live with his wife in a separate dwelling. This form of marriage was still prevalent as late as the 1980s in villages scattered throughout the Jaintia Hills, the region adjacent to the Khasi Hills. In matrilocal or uxorilocal marriage, the husband is largely at the mercy of his wife's family, as either his wife or his mother-in-law is "lord of the house." The man remains "somebody's son," and his family history is of no consequence. The same form of marriage exists among the Garos, however their system grants men considerably more rights. Women own the house and property, but the husband may take full advantage of both. Most importantly perhaps is that he may continue to use his wife's house and property in the event of her death. The relatives of the deceased are even obliged to provide him with a new wife—naturally from the same clan. The lack of men's rights in Khasi society corresponds to the legal position of the *khadduh* described above. The *khadduh*'s duty to preserve the ancestral heritage is supported by her maternal uncle or her brother (*kni*). His position is even more important than that of her husband, for the *kni* oversees the work in the fields and the children's upbringing and education.

With husbands having so few rights divorce is not uncommon in matrilocal marriages. Since no financial demands are made of the father with regard to the children, who always remain with their mother, divorce never ends in financial disaster for the woman. The husband

Left and below: *Young Khasis in traditional costumes.*

usually simply returns to his maternal family.

The Neolocal Marriage

This modern form of family life allows husbands somewhat more freedom. It is practiced by Christian Khasi couples and is intended to relieve the man of the pressures that are traditionally put on him. The newly-weds build their own hut or house in the same village as the bride's maternal family, but remain quite independent thereof. If the wife is not the heir of the property, that is, is not a *khadduh*, then the husband is not only entitled to use the property but also becomes co-owner of it. This is why Khasi men prefer to marry non-heirs, since those women will not have a dowry that would enable them to live independently of their husbands. In this form of Khasi marriage the *khadduh* is still the only person entitled to inherit from the "neolocal" couple in the event of their death.

The Virilocal Marriage

This extremely rare form of marriage is practiced only among the young Christianized intellectuals of Meghalaya's capital, Shillong, according to which the woman moves into the newly founded house of her husband and accepts him as the head of the family.

With such strict, female-oriented family structures, polygamy is not a rare consequence among the Khasis. Husbands who are not entitled to inherit are free to take a second wife, who, however, is not allowed to enter the house of the first wife, for women from different clans are forbidden to share the same house or work together. Thus the man goes from house to house, keeping his maternal family as his base. This practice is becoming increasingly widespread among the Khasis, despite the objections raised by the Christian Church. Taking a second wife is also quite common in Garo society, in which the husband is legally obliged to marry his mother-in-law in the event of his father-in-law's death. Moreover if a husband takes a second wife, he may take her to his first wife's house, but the different status of the women is made perfectly clear. The second wife is called the "stolen wife" and her offspring referred to as the "children from the fork of the family" (*ki khun kliar*), as opposed to

the offspring of the first wife, who are called the "children of the root" (*khun trai*). The former are naturally not entitled to inherit unless they are adopted by the first wife, which is done when she herself has had no daughters.[2]

The few rights of men in a Khasi family contrasts with the wide range of sociological functions and duties they must fulfill. Traditionally the man was obliged to protect the clan by defending it in the event of war. Moreover the government administration and state representation in the Indian Union is solely the responsibility of Khasi men, who hold most political positions, as mayors, priests, village heads or campaign managers, to name a few. The most important positions as seen from the outside are those of the 25 *syiems*, consisting of monarchs, chiefs and mayors, who represent the 25 Khasi districts. Yet their power is granted to them by a woman: *Syiem sad*, the high priestess of the village of Smit near Shillong, who chooses the *syiems* from among her sons, nephews and other male relatives.

Khasi men's reactions to women's hegemony in society is diverse. On the one hand

Two Meithei imas, or "mothers," from Manipur, who help put on the market of the same name in the state's capital, Imphal. Only elderly women, who are past their childbearing years are permitted to take part in it.

Members of the Synkhong Rympei Thymmai, the "Society of the New Hearth," Meghalaya's, and indeed the world's, first and only men's emancipation movement.

A Meithei ima *in the evening light at Kwairamband Bazaar.*

Below left: *"We imas are a big family. Here at the market we sit together and discuss our problems. I am still healthy and strong. Why should I stay at home? As long as I can be here at the bazaar I am happy."*

Below right: *If a son is born in a Meithei household, his relatives visit him on the twentieth day after his birth, showering him with gifts, food and toys.*

men acknowledge and appreciate women's capabilities and consider it a laudable achievement that, in their society, under the leadership of women, poverty and homeless people do not exist. The men are aware of the fact that the tasks and responsibilities are directed toward the women and acknowledge the historical reason for this fact: in Khasi society it has always been considered beneficial for families to be run by women since the men's traditional role was to hunt and wage war, which put their lives at risk. Most Khasi men do not view themselves as having few rights since questions and decisions are discussed and their opinions are always taken into consideration. Thus they reject "matriarchy" as a description of their social system, a term meaning that the women have absolute power. The dominance of the *khadduh* in the Khasi family rather depends on the transfer of property and the religious rank of the woman. For this reason they prefer to use the term "matrilineality." On the other hand Shillong is the only place on earth where a male emancipation movement has taken place over the past few years. It is called the "Society of the New Hearth" and has some

1,000 members, who object to men's lack of property, their purpose as "breeding studs" and the role they must play in the wife's maternal family, which they describe as "remaining an eternal alien." They condemn unequal treatment.
If money is scarce, for example, only daughters are allowed to attend school. Furthermore in many families in which only male heirs exist, it is deemed preferable to adopt a girl instead of passing on the property to a son. The spreading Christianization in Meghalaya supports the men's emancipation movement. Most institutions of higher education are run by Christians and the curriculum taught there only rarely draws on traditional values. For now it remains uncertain whether the Khasis' matrilineal society will survive the onslaught of men's demands for equal treatment and a religion whose god is male.

Though unquestionable unique, Meghalaya is not the only place in which women are strong in Northeast India. Most of the peoples of the region, no matter how patriarchal their communities are, attach great importance to women and their roles in society. The Meitheis of

Manipur are one example, although Meithei women had to fight hard for their rights. In the so-called Nupilan Revolution (nupi = woman; lan = war) in 1939, when they rebelled against being economically and politically oppressed by the British as well as Manipuri men. In addition to founding the women's party Nisha Bandh, which still exists today, the Ima Market was initiated at the Kwairamband Bazaar in Imphal, Manipur's capital. Every day, from 7 a.m. to 7 p.m., this fascinating event is restaged by some 3,000 proud women of at least 45 years of age (ima = mother) who offer a wide range of wares, including colorful fabrics, food, pottery and tools. Imas would not dream of haggling over their wares as is customary in other parts of India. Their notions of price are warranted, for the quality of the items sold here is extremely high. Not only is the family income supplemented by the money earned by these middle-aged to elderly women, but the relationship between mother- and daughter-in-laws have been considerably improved, for, when the "old ones" are at work, mothers have greater freedom with regard to carrying out household activities and raising children.[3]

Women enjoy such a high status among the Padam-Adis of Arunachal Pradesh that a bridegroom, together with his family, must recompense the bride's family for the loss of their daughter during an entire lifetime by paying continual installments in the form of partial harvests or hunting bounty, as a sort of long-term dowry.[4] It would perhaps seem as though women were treated like property that is bought and owned, yet the reality for women looks different. This is reflected in the relatively loose attitude of the native peoples taken toward premarital sex. Since it is assumed that, without divine consent, no "proper" relationship can be formed, engaging in sex before being married is only superficially taboo. If a woman bears one or more illegitimate children, they are unreservedly adopted by her husband when she marries. This "free" premarital period gives adolescents a chance to get to know each other and to find suitable partners. Although marriages are arranged in almost all Northeast Indian societies, parents take their children's wishes into account when choosing a spouse for them, so that even with dowry payments, the basis of men and women living together is love, not material wealth.[5] Like so many aspects of Northeast

Right: An Adi-Pasi bride on her wedding day. She wears an old Tibetan bowl on her head like a crown, a sign of wealth in Adi society and, for the parents, a symbol of recompense for the loss of their daughter. Photograph: G. Horter.

Below: A precious silver bowl of Tibetan origin, used as part of a dowry at an Adi wedding. Photograph: A. Nath.

Bottom: A very rare sight of an "army" of Gallong-Adi women "soldiers"! The parading of the all-women army at occasional festivals does not have folkloric origins but can be traced back to the long tradition of war among the Adis. These women form the final human bulwark of their village should their men lose their lives at war. They demonstrate their equality with men, even in their ability to fight. Photograph: A. Nath.

Indian societies, the importance attached to the role of women in the community often draws on myth or religious concepts, transforming them into social customs. Many creation myths state that, in the beginning, the primal being was female, such as a Singpho myth that states: *"From the great primal mist came the Universal Mother."* According to indigenous belief, natural phenomena have sexual overtones: "lightning is the flashing of the Divine Mother's eyelids" (Minyong-Adi). Less common, though just as revealing, is the idea that the sun is feminine: "The sun is a woman, always hot with desire and shining brightly" (Singpho). Furthermore a Digaru-Mishmi story humorously attributes the more positive characteristics of the sun to the female sex: "The sun has both sexes. When it is a woman the day is long; when it is a man he quickly disappears to rest at home." Among the Noctes and the Moklum-Tangsas only women are said to have inhabited the earth in the beginning of the world. This notion recurs frequently in Northeast Indian mythology, which in itself indicates the special status enjoyed by women. The Hill Miris and the Sherdukpens believe that there is a fastness in the mountains where only women live. "These women possess all the world's gold, silver and iron as well as sacred beads, bells and priceless swords."[6]

The belief in and importance of female divinities as an overriding principle is common to all Northeast Indian peoples; it leaves its mark on all aspects of cultural life, be it textiles, architecture, megaliths, sacrificial cults, head-hunting or the many creation myths and notions of the divine. In this part of the world concepts that might well have at one time characterized the worldview of prehistoric societies are still alive. Here it is still believed that cosmic forces are united in the female body, that woman is nature incarnate. Her entire being is associated with the celestial bodies: in menstruating she is connected to the phases of the moon; in giving birth she is identified with the rising sun, both of which are symbols of waxing and waning, birth and death. The mysterious and powerful red color of such natural

phenomena as the sun or fire and flowers and fruit, which harbor the capacity of creating new life next spring—all these are seen to reflect women's monthly cycle and childbirth. Just as the red sun, when it sets promises a new day, so too does the blood of menstruation and birth herald renewal or the processes through which new life can emerge. By giving birth the circle of blood relatives is enlarged. Life on earth is enriched by the birth of new member of the family and the mother carries on the life-giving principle of the female deity, the Primal Mother.

That the processes unfolding inside a woman's body follow the same cycles as such natural phenomena as the phases of the moon, the seasons and, by symbolic extension, the rhythm of day and night is regarded as proof of the harmony that exists between women and the cosmos. Women are seen as the carriers of life, death and rebirth. She is seen as the "keeper of the divine," as the path to oneness with the omnipotent principle.

Thus it is not far-fetched to imagine the divine principle, whose physical embodiment is assumed to be woman, as being female. The notion of the Great Mother combines three aspects of femininity that are ascertainable everywhere, but are perhaps nowhere more obvious than in Northeast India:

1) the human mother, who gives birth, nourishes, preserves the household's fire and prepares food (the ability to distinguish between good and bad food is equated with possessing knowledge and wisdom),

2) the ancestral mother, who unites birth, life, death and rebirth,

3) and, finally, the Cosmic Mother, who is the cosmogonic keeper, nourisher and preserver of everything eternal and immortal.

In this concept man is superior to woman only in his physical abilities: he can build houses, ward off danger, kill animals and wage war. Yet man is born of woman and is not capable of carrying on human life beyond his own. This function lies exclusively with woman, be it in her transient earthly existence or in her symbolic being as the Great Mother.[7]

Many notions about the divine in Northeast India derive from this understanding of womanhood. When head-hunting was still common, women's heads were more highly prized than men's among the Sema-Nagas since they were thought to contain the

Top: *Calm and content, this Garo mother smiles into the camera, conscious of her powerful position in society.* Bottom: *A Mogh girl from Tripura dressed and made up for her stay in the village monastery.*

essence of the female soul, which was believed to have the highest fertility value. To this day the prayers of Tripuri shamans usually end with "O Mother, I pray to you so that you grant my prayers!" Many high deities are believed to be female, be they benevolent or malevolent. For the Uchais of Tripura it is the river goddess, Tuima—"the Mother"—who ensures the well-being of humans if she is properly appeased, that is, if the correct sacrifices are made.[8]

The assumption that the deity must be appeased suggests that she can be vengeful. This idea finds its clearest expression in the Kali cult of the Assamese Hindus, in which, to this day, some of the most ancient of religious concepts have survived. Eastern India, with its present-day states of Bihar, West Bengal and Assam, has always been the seat of Tantric Hinduism and Buddhism. The term (from Sanskrit: tan = "thread"), meaning as much as fabric, alludes to the interrelationships existing between all things.[9] Tantric practices are not limited to a specific religion and involve customs that can be traced back to a time predating the emergence of the so-called world religions.

They encompass magical formulas and invocations (mantras), magical diagrams (yantras), meditation models (mandalas) and physical exercises (yoga), especially of a sexual nature. It is believed that, by employing these mystical aids, the lengthy process of birth, death and reincarnation leading to enlightenment may be shortened, making it possible to break the sorrowful cycle of reincarnation within one lifetime. Sexual potency and the life force are regarded as the quintessential and most powerful impulses of all cosmic and therefore also earthly processes. On the one hand these quintessential forces can be used to engender new life. On the other hand they are viewed as the strongest power by which salvation may be attained if its potential is used in a transcendent, spiritual manner.[10] Tantric concepts have found their way into the art of Northeast India, either in a purely abstract form—that is, by reducing the basic principles of the dualistic cosmos to stylized depictions of genitalia (lingam = phallus; yoni = vagina)—or as highly symbolic depictions of wrathful deities straddling animals and holding numerous body parts in their

hands. A well-known example of the latter type is Kali, the bloodthirsty and furious goddess of destruction, who is frequently shown holding severed heads in her myriad hands and who demands that human beings perform sacrifices to her. This version of the female divine principle is relatively old (from the fourth millennium B.C.) and demonstrates that the religions of the indigenous peoples have continued to evolve. The principle of the Primal Mother may still be discerned, yet now she must constantly be appeased, which was probably not believed in prehistoric times.

The reason for this might have been the development of a dualistic worldview in Hinduism (as well as other religions): the paradisiacal primordial world was broken down into opposites. Knowledge of good and bad did not only involve recognizing the differences between the sexes but also led to fear, such as man being afraid of

Shiva as "Lord of the Soil" at the Hayagriva temple in Hajo, Assam. The phallic lingam, located in front of the deity's head, symbolizes the god's fertility powers in the earth's soil.

Kamakshya temple on Nilachal Hill in Gauhati, Assam, the most sacred of temples for members of the Shakti cult.

woman's life-giving powers, which did not repel him in his preconscious state; quite to the contrary, he felt at one with it. In order to make the female powers benevolent, they now had to be appeased. The best way to accomplish this was to offer sacrifices involving blood, since, through the ages, blood had been associated with life. Thus arose the associations between goddess, blood, soil and fertility.

In the earliest fertility cults the sacrificial offerings after invoking a deity were cut into pieces, whereupon they were buried in the earth—an act of returning fertility to the soil, or earthly womb, from which it was thought to come (as may be seen in symbolic form also among the Nagas). Through this act the soil brought in contact with the maternal, therefore omnipotent, principle of blood was thought to be fecundated again, ensuring the survival of the community.

This notion of fertility being absolutely

essential for survival grew ever more pronounced over time. Fertility was believed to exist only if Kali was furious and actively destructive. Thus the life-engendering force was equated with death and all opposites were now assumed to be reflections of the same principle. Even if, or as soon as, the goddess destroyed everything around her, new life would spring from her womb. This makes destruction, or sacrifice, a purification process and blood a symbol of renewal and regeneration. Thus Kali symbolizes purity. In a transcendental sense, worshipping her gives rise to purification from all negative aspects that deter the adept from attaining enlightenment.[11]

The largest temple devoted to the Mother Goddess, Kali, or Kamakshya in Assam (also Durga, Parvati, Shakti or Sita), is the largest temple on Nilachal Hill in Gauhati. The creation myth associated with the site reveals what an integral part sacrificial cults are to this Indian religion:

Kamakshya, the Mother Goddess in her incarnation as Sati, was the wife of Shiva, the god of destruction. She had married the wild god on the condition that none of the divinities would ever

cause her offense, otherwise she would throw herself into the fire and Shiva would avenge the world. One day, during a great sacrificial ceremony, Daksha, the son of Brahma, the world's Preserver, began to speak badly about Shiva. What he said made Sati very angry, so she threw herself into the sacrificial fire. Shiva awoke from his eternal meditation. Furious he flung himself on Daksha and his following, killed them and, with his wife's listless body draped over his shoulders, began to destroy everything in sight. Brahma and Vishnu (the Creator) knew that Shiva would be assuaged once Sati's body had vanished. Therefore Vishnu used his wheel of death to cut up Sati's body and scatter it around the world. He cut her into fifty-one pieces, and every place where a piece of her body fell became a sacred site. The place where Sati's womb fell to earth became the most sacred places of pilgrimage of all. It was on Nilachal Hill in Gauhati.[12]

According to the *Puranas* forty of the fifty-one *pithashthans*, places where pieces of Sati's body fell to earth, are located in

Above: *Inside the temple complex a pilgrim with a black statue of Kamakshya, also known as Kali, adorned with red flowers and garments symbolizing the blood, or fertility, of the deity. The tridents are symbols of Kali's husband, Shiva. The temple grounds are covered with a mixture consisting of sacrificial blood, the urine of the animals used in daily sacrifices—such as goats, rams and doves—and rain water collected during the monsoon season.*

Left: *Stone carving (Imphal Museum, Manipur) of the Meithei sun and fertility goddess. From her vagina appears a tiger, a symbol of strength and power.*

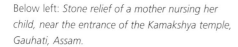

Below left: *Stone relief of a mother nursing her child, near the entrance of the Kamakshya temple, Gauhati, Assam.*

Below center: *This sculpture in Gauhati's Kamakshya temple illustrates how central the life-engendering womb is to Assamese Hinduism.*

Below: *This picture of the deity Hayagriva in the temple in Hajo, Assam, shows the atmosphere inside temples connected to the Kamakshya-Kali cult. They are usually dark and gloomy, giving an impression of foreboding.*

India. The remaining eleven are found in Nepal, Bangladesh, Pakistan and Sri Lanka. This myth reveals just how important the Kamakshya temple is for worshipping the Mother-Goddess, that Kamakshya represents in Assamese Hinduism, for what other part of the body is more central to motherhood than the womb? To this day it is considered to be the most sacred of temples by the members of the Shakti cult, who continue to venerate the female principle and who believe that all creation has its origin in the womb of a female deity.

Once a year the female principle of the Mother Goddess can be physically experienced at Kamakshya temple when the fountains there turn red. It is believed that during this time Kamakshya menstruates, which is why the temple is closed, for menstruation is associated with impurity, when all that is old, decaying and evil is discarded, calling for the observance of certain taboos. All work in the fields is stopped in Assam (for menstruation is an infertile period) and the devout rest. After three days a large festival is held, marking the end of the period of abstinence. For four days the *devadasis*, or virgin temple dancers, perform inside the complex. The purity of Kamakshya is believed to be most intense now, which is passed on to the dancers who are initiated in a lengthy ceremony. The dancers begin their performance slowly, dancing to the beat of drums and the sound of conch shells being played. Gradually the momentum builds until the dancers are worked up into a state of ecstasy, possessed by the Mother Goddess herself. What the *devadasis* foretell in this state is thought to come true. Men are not permitted to watch these performances, for it is believed that, by doing so, they would immediately turn to stone (as is said to have happened to an Ahom king who insisted on witnessing the spectacle).[13]

The innermost sanctuary of the Kamakshya temple lies within a dark cave beneath the main temple. It consists of a stone *yoni*, the Hindu symbol of the female sex, which is covered with innumerable flower garlands and silk saris. When descending the many steps that lead to the sanctuary one cannot deny having the rather strange impression that one is indeed returning to the mother's womb. This may be caused in part by the heat and high humidity of the sacred site.

Kamakshya veneration is reserved exclusively for those who have been initiated into the Shakti cult, which has always been one of the most esoteric and personal forms of worship in India. Its origins and teachings are documented in extraordinary sacramental and magical scriptures, the *Mahanirvana Tantra*, whose content remains unintelligible to the uninitiated. There are autonomous schools within Hinduism that concern themselves exclusively with their interpretation and application. Yet it is clear that Shaktism (*shakti* denotes "creative force") is an amalgamation of Hindu and indigenous ideas of the people in Eastern India.

Beyond the walls of the temple the people of Assam also pay tribute to female fertility by celebrating Bihu, the annual spring festival, which embraces the primal desire for fertility, survival and growth. It lasts for about a week, starting with the first rain and the blossoming of (blood red) flowers. People dance, play drums and sing, cakes are baked and relatives are visited. The first day is devoted to celebrating domestic animals. Buffaloes are bathed, adorned with garlands made from vegetables and a curcuma and black lentil paste is applied to their horns. Only every four years is a white buffalo sacrificed—it would seem that the people have chosen to celebrate the part of Kali's powers that give life instead of taking it.

Yet, the blood cult has not yet been completely extinguished. This is on account of Northeast India's cultural history, which, surprisingly, can be traced to the civilization of ancient Egypt. Since human sacrifice has always been considered the highest possible means of attaining the principle of fertility, traditionally it went hand in hand with the Kali cult. Curiously a close link also exists between human sacrifice and head-hunting: When, in 1565, the Assamese king Narnarayana consecrated the Kamakshya temple by sacrificing 140 men, he placed their heads in front of the temple on copper plates. One of his successors, King Raghu of Gaolpara, Kamrup and Darrang, sacrificed as many as 700 men to Kamakshya, many of whom are purported to have volunteered to die, and offered their heads to the deity.[14]

Conversely, at the Tripuran festival of *Kharchi puja*, which is held every year in June and July at Old Agartala, the heads of 14 deities are venerated. Every likeness of the deities includes two horns behind the crowns, which the following Assamese myth explains: *Once, while fetching water from a mountain stream, the Mother Goddess Harabati, heard voices calling out "Mother, Mother, save us!" They were the voices of fourteen deities who were resting on the branches of a shimul tree. They had been attacked by a vicious buffalo. Harabati protected them from the beast and had it killed by her men. The deities came down from the tree and drank the animal's blood. Their fondness of blood persisted, even when they were enshrined in the palace of the Mother Goddess, where a he goat had to be sacrificed to them every night.*[15]

The heads of the fourteen deities have been dated on stylistic grounds to between the 13th and the 15th centuries.[16] Before the reign of King Govinda Manikya, in the mid-17th century, human sacrifices were frequently made to the gods.[17] Since the aforementioned myth does not refer to human sacrifice, but instead to that of animals, it must date from a later period. As we have seen, this transferal, from humans to animals, is described in the Aka

myth quoted in the chapter titled "I am the Tiger." Thus the symbolic meaning of the horns appearing behind the crowns of the deities could be interpreted as the ancient fertility symbols that have always been used in tribal societies to adorn the persons depicted. Yet it is peculiar that only the heads are worshipped. Does this perhaps suggest a connection to the head-hunting practices of the Nagas? A closer look at the idols reveals that they all relate to human fertility and well-being.[18] Thus parallels between head-hunting and human sacrifice can certainly be drawn since the aim of both was to acquire the essence of the soul, the omnipotent principle of fertility, which was deemed necessary for the well-being and survival of a community.

Such benefits did not necessarily have to be of a collective kind. Among the Jaintias of Meghalaya it was common, even during British occupation, to offer human sacrifices to secure a personal wish, such as the birth of a child. Until the 1950s the Khasis used to sacrifice human beings to the snake god, U Thlen (the snake being a symbol of the Mother Goddess). This custom, which involved black magic, was supposed to free a family from the influence of the deity and make it prosper. Until the reign of Rudra Singh (1696–1714), it was common practise among Assamese kings to sacrifice men with the ancestral sword, which was believed to be the tongue of the Mother Goddess Kamakshya, was common practice.[19]

Evidence also exists of head-hunting peoples in former times having made human sacrifices. During the harvesting ceremony of the Angami-Nagas two phallic posts are erected in front of the porch of the house of the man on whose behalf the feast is held. They then push a victim off the roof of the house, nowadays a puppy, which is equipped with human trappings, such as a spear and a garment. Traditionally, however, the victims were human beings. The Konyak-Nagas sacrificed humans such that the blood ran onto a ladder that led to the house of the person performing the sacrifice. The Ao-Nagas used to offer men to the spirit Tsungrem, who was believed to be the cause of all illnesses.[20] Such bloody customs have led anthropologists to ask whether cannibalism was also prevalent among the peoples of Northeast India. Of the few remaining vestiges of such practices that

had survived in this region was a custom of the Jaintias in Meghalaya, whose royal family, after a successful battle, partook of a small quantity of rice cooked in the blood of the enemy.[21] Similarly, if a quarrel broke out between members of the various Garo clans, both parties would plant a tree bearing a sour fruit and solemnly swear that they would avenge their enemy at the first possible opportunity by eating its fruit with the juice of their enemy's head. The person who succeeded in capturing his enemy cut off the latter's head, summoned his friends, with whom he boiled the head along with the fruit of the tree, and shared the mixture with them. The tree was then cut down and the feud ended. The Mizos used to taste the liver of the first victim

Top: *An Aka mother meditating on a stone as a source of fertility.* Bottom: *The* morung *tradition in Naga societies enables lifelong ties to form.*

slain in war and lick his blood from the spearhead. After a successful head-hunt the Thadou-Kukis ate a meal with hands still covered with the blood of their enemies.[22] Moreover the custom of the Apa Tanis of Arunachal Pradesh of biting persons in the village pillory suggests cannibalistic tendencies. Among the Sema-Nagas a returning head-hunter had to eat at least one morsel of food before entering his village. This was done with bloody hands, for he was not allowed to wash them until after having had his meal. Certainly the idea was to transfer the essence of the victim's soul to the hunter.

The principle connecting head-hunting, human sacrifice and cannibalism is the desire to acquire the essence of the soul, the fertility power, which was regarded as being a female attribute. Each of these traditions was practiced just as it had been for centuries, in accordance with what was

perceived to be the divine cosmic law suffusing all things.

In Northeast India the remnants of the archaic world are not revealed to us in paintings, sculptures or archaeological remains only, as it is common for other parts of the world, but in the customs and traditions of the peoples themselves, whose lifestyles have remained almost unchanged for centuries. Observing these peoples' ways of life sheds considerable light on ancient civilizations, such as predynastic Egypt, Crete, Asia Minor and Mesopotamia, all of which embraced the notion of a Mother Goddess, which in fact originated in Egypt among a group of people that called themselves "the children of the sun."[23] Yet the earliest depictions of the fertility goddess date from the Paleolithic age, when she was portrayed with exaggeratedly large hips, breasts and genitalia. Anthropologists believe that this ideal image of female beauty was derived from the shape of the cowry shell, which has been a symbol of fertility and birth since time immemorial.[24] Curiously cowry shells have retained precisely this meaning among certain Naga peoples, who fix them to textiles of a highly symbolic nature, intended to be worn by fertile members of the community.[25] Moreover ever since she was conceived, the Mother Goddess has been associated with snakes. In Sumer one of her names was "mother great serpent." A similar belief, especially in connection with human sacrifice, was held by the Khasis and their customs regarding U Thlen, the snake god.

It has always been agricultural fertility that has been most readily associated with the Mother Goddess. In the ancient civilizations of Egypt and Asia Minor, too, the highest offerings possible to attain this fertility were believed to be those that involved blood—at first by means of human, then animal, sacrifice. The notion of the highest deity being female has in one way or another left its mark on the concepts underlying all Northeast Indian societies. Traces of this ancient concept can even still be found among such peoples as the Nagas, who view themselves as being strictly patriarchal: among the Angamis the name of the supreme deity, U Kepneopfa, is feminine. The Zumomi clan of the Sema-Nagas traces its descent to an ancestress called Putheli.[27] Matrilineal societies are not only common among the Khasis and the Garos, though they have certainly

preserved it in its purest and most distinctive form. Traces of matrilineal society are also discernible among the Semas and other Naga clans in which maternal uncles are still shown great respect. Among the Lakhers a close relationship exists between the maternal uncle and his nephews and nieces, of which the former is treated with great respect. All payments due to a given family, such as dowries or death payments, are entrusted with the maternal uncle. The most highly respected title among this people is not *ipa*, denoting "father," but *papu*, signifying "uncle," a name that is extended to Lakher chiefs.[28] The Hill Miris have only recently become patrilineal and therefore still display elements of a matrilineal system. As if to emphasize the change and to show that the father has a close relationship with his children, the father acts like a second mother, going through the motions of a mock childbirth, the so-called "couvade". He lies in bed for forty days after the birth of the child and, during this period, he is fed like an invalid.[29] As it is customary among the Adis, Hill Miri bridegrooms must first serve in the house of the bride's mother.[30] The Thadou-Kukis have a tradition of making what are called "bone payments" for keeping the bones of a mother or her child in the husband's family. It is presumed that, if the bones were returned, the soul would, in the life to come, remain with the mother's relatives. It is conceivable that the "bone payment" is akin to the Khasi custom whereby the bones of the whole matrilineal clan are occasionally collected during an important religious ceremony. Similarly the Lhota-Nagas have a payment called the *echiman*, or "death payment," which can be accompanied by a payment called *ming eshi*, or "name payment," which entitles the family of the payer to use the dead woman's name for children born in subsequent generations.[31] Phallic rites and adornments (such as documenting successful head-hunts in tattoos or carvings) that are traditionally associated with the cult of the Great Mother were common in most Naga, Mizo and Kuki societies. Even "modernized" Northeast Indian societies still reveal aspects of ancient civilizations in which the Mother Goddess was venerated: the splitting of one clan into two, for example, which carries sexual connotations. This social organization is not only encountered among the Ao-, Sema-,

Mao-, Thangkhul-, Angami- and Konyak-Nagas,[32] but also the Tai Ahoms of Assam.[33] The Aka myth described in the chapter titled "I am the Tiger" may also have evolved during a time when the Akas sought to switch from a matriarchal to a patriarchal society, though it seems to be a myth that is intended to perpetuate this people's traditional social system.

This state of cultural flux may be felt far and wide in Northeast India. The signs and expressions of the ancient culture rooted in the worship of the Mother Goddess are still encountered here. Yet, owing to the increased means of communication, the opening of the region to foreign influence and the enhanced relations between the various indigenous peoples living here, change is occurring rapidly—change that for some will no doubt be beneficial, for others will prove to be difficult to adjust to and for others still will most certainly spell the end.

The forest closed behind us, shutting the valley in, shutting us out, and we walked forward through the centuries. . .toward the alien and bitter present and the strangers who were our kind. . . .Willing or not, we had eaten from the Tree of Knowledge, and we had realized that, across barriers of caste and color, human beings are one—all struggling along the same dark road . . .
Ursula Graham Bower[34]

Among the Laju-Noctes of Arunachal Pradesh, as in many tribal societies, the grandmother is still the true head of the family, even in patrilineal societies.

Footnotes

Introduction:
1: Quinn, 2: Elwin: Nagaland

Chapter 1: The Seven Sisters of India
1: Elwin: Art, 2: Izzard, 3: Whitehead, 4: Kowall, 5: Bower: Hidden land, 6: Elwin: Philosophy, 7: Fürer-Haimendorf: Himalayan Barbary, 8: Verghese.

Chapter 2: The Indigenous Peoples of Northeast India and their Origins
1: Singh: a), 2: Chowdhury, 3: Singh: d), 4: Singh: e), 5: Singh: b), 6: Singh: c), 7: Singh: a), 8: Chowdhury, 9: Choudhury, 10: Singh: f), 11: Chowdhury, 12: Choudhury, 13: Das, R., 14: Choudhury, 15: Chowdhury, 16: Singh: e), 17: Elwin: Myths, 18: Pakrasi, 19: Chowdhury, 20: Singh: a), 21: Singh: d), 22: Singh: e), 23: Chowdhury, 24-27: Singh: a), 28: Jacobs, 29: Singh: a), 30: Niyogi, 31: Singh: e).

Chapter 3: The Apa Tanis
1: Chowdhury , 2: Compiled from: Bower: Hidden land, Fürer-Haimendorf: Himalayan Barbary, Singh: a), Fürer-Haimendorf: Himalayan tribe.

Chapter 4: The Peoples of the Sun and Moon
1: Singh: a), 2: Singh: e), 3: Jacobs, 4: Bertrand, 5: Gerlitz, 6: Singh: f), 7: Sandys, 8: Bhattacharjee, 9: Singh: f), 10: Choudhury, 11: Doshi, 12, 13: Elwin: World, 14: Riba.

Chapter 5: The House – The Womb
1: Kükelhaus, 2-4: Chowdhury, 5: Elwin: World

Chapter 6: In Heaven as on Earth
1: Elwin: Philosophy, 2-5: Compiled from: Elwin: Art, Naga Institute, Barbier, Das, A.K.

Chapter 7: All is Color and Motion
1: Elwin: World, 2: Compiled from: Khokar, Madeisky & Werner.

Chapter 8: Poetry, Devotion and Strength
1: Levine, 2: Compiled from Doshi, Constantine, Hodson: Meitheis.

Chapter 9: Words of the Shaman
1: Borgohain & Chaudhury, 2: Singh: a), 3: Varman, 4-7: Singh: a), 8: Madeisky & Werner, 9: Singh: a), 10: Jacobs, 11: Singh: a), 12: Thanga, 13: Singh: a), 14: Varman, 15: Kowall, 16: Ham, 17, 18: Singh: a), 19: Sema, 20: Singh: a).

Chapter 10: High Religion and Magicians
1: Rinpungpa, 2: Singh: a), 3: Compiled from Schicklgruber, Dalai Lama, Peissel, 4: Singh: a), 5: Robinson, 6, 7: Chowdhury, 8: Peissel, 9: Singh: a), 10: Compiled from Ham & Stirn: Buddhas, Ham & Stirn: Forgotten Gods, 11: Chowdhury, 12, 13: Varman, 14: Singh: f), 15: Bhattacharjee.

Chapter 11: "I am the Tiger, the Buffalo is my Sister"
1: Elwin: Myths, 2: Fürer-Haimendorf: Himalayan Adventure, 3: Jacobs, 4: Bhattacharjee, 5: Borgohain & Chaudhury, 6: Singh: a), 7: Thansanga, 8: Sangma, 9: Jacobs, 10: Jacobs, 11: Sangma and the authors' informant Nesfield Sangma, Tura, Meghalaya, 12: Jacobs, 13: Singh: a), 14: Singh: e), 15: Luczak, 16: Singh: a).

Chapter 12: Fertility through Stones and Heads
1: Jacobs, 2: Compiled from Gerlitz, Madeisky & Werner, Luczak, 3: Compiled from Thanga, Sangkima, Lalrimawia, 4: Thanga, 5: Bhattacharjee, 6: Das, R., 7: Jacobs, 8: Compiled from Jacobs and Schuster & Carpenter, 9: Jacobs, 10: Gohain, 11: Compiled from Gohain, Jacobs, Singh: e), 12: Jacobs, 13: Bhattacharjee, 14, 15: Jacobs, 16: Elwin: Art, 24: Jacobs, 17: Chowdhury, 18: Nalin, 19: Compiled from Chowdhury and Singh: a).

Chapter 13: Women's Mysterious Realm
1: Madeisky & Werner, 2: Compiled from Gerlitz, 3: Compiled from Constantine and Doshi, 4: Singh: a), 5: Chowdhury, 6: Compiled from: Elwin: Myths, 7: Uhlig, 8: Bhattacharjee, 9: Uhlig, 10: Ham & Stirn: Forgotten Gods,

11: Compiled from Uhlig and Heine-Geldern, 12: Heine-Geldern, 13: Compiled from Choudhury and Heine-Geldern, 14: Gohain, 15: Bhattacharjee, 16: Das, R., 17: Heine-Geldern, 18: Bhattacharjee, 19-22: Compiled from Gohain and Heine-Geldern, 23: Uhlig, 24-29: Compiled from Gohain and Heine-Geldern, 30: Singh: a), 31: Gohain, 32: Jacobs, 33: Gohain, 34: Bower: Hidden land.

Bibliography

Bahadur, M., Y. Santabai, *Tribal Art of Manipur*, Imphal 1989

Barbier, J. P., *Art of Nagaland*, Geneva 1984

Bernard, P., *Les Oubliées du Temps*, Xonrupt-Lomgemer 1988

Bernard, P., M. Huteau, *Nagaland: Les Frontières de l'espoir*, Fontenay-sous-Bois 1990 (documentary film)

— *Meghalaya: Le Domaine des Nuages*, Fontenay-sous-Bois 1990 (documentary film)

Bertrand, G., *Geheimnisvolles Reich der Frauen. Zwei Jahre bei den tibetanischen Stämmen in Assam*, Zurich 1957

Bhattacharjee, P., *Tribal Pujas and Festivals in Tripura*, Agartala 1994

Borgohain, B. K., P. C. Roy Chaudhury, *Folk Tales of Nagaland, Manipur, Tripura and Assam*, New Delhi 1991

Bower, U. G., *Naga Path*, London 1952

— *The Hidden Land*, London 1953

Brauns, C. D.; L. G. Löffler, *Mru. Bergbewohner im Grenzgebiet von Bangladesh*. Basel, Boston, Stuttgart 1986

Carey, B. S., H. N. Tuck, *The Chin Hills. A History of the People, our Dealings with them, their Customs and Manners, and a Gazeteer of their Country* , Rangoon 1896

Choudhury, P. C., *The history of civilisation of the people of Assam to the twelfth century A.D.*, Gauhati 1959

Chowdhury, J. N., *Arunachal Panorama. A Study in Profile*, Itanagar 1992

Constantine, R., *Manipur, Maid of the Mountains*, New Delhi 1981.

Dalai Lama, *Freedom in Exile*, London 1990.

Dalton, E. T., *A Descriptive Ethnology of Bengal*, Calcutta 1872.

Das, A. K. *Tribal Art and Craft*, Delhi 1979.

Das, R., *Art and Architecture of Tripura*, Agartala 1997

Doshi, S., *Dances of Manipur. The Classical Tradition*, Bombay 1989

Dutta, P., *The Noctes*, Shillong 1978

— *The Wanchos*, Naharlagun 1990

Elwin, V., *Myths of the North-East Frontier of India*, Shillong 1957

— *A Philosphy for NEFA*, Shillong 1957

— *The Art of the North-East Frontier of India*, Shillong 1958

— *Nagaland*, Shillong 1961

— *When the World was young. Folk Tales from India's Hills and Forests*, New Delhi 1961

— *A New Book on Tribal Fiction*, Shillong 1963

Fürer-Haimendorf, C. v.: *Die Nackten Nagas*, Leipzig 1939

— *Himalayan Barbary*, London 1955

— *Return to the Naked Nagas*, London 1976

— *A Himalayan Tribe. From Cattle to Cash*, Berkeley and Los Angeles 1980

— *Himalayan Adventure. Early Travels in North East India*, New Delhi 1983

Gerlitz, P., *Religion und Matriarchat. Zur religionsgeschichtlichen Bedeutung der matrilinearen Strukturen bei den Khasi von Meghalaya unter besonderer Berücksichtigung der national-religiösen Reformbewegungen. Studies in Oriental Religions*, Vol. 11. Bonn 1984

Gohain, B. C., *Human sacrifice and Head-hunting in North Eastern India*, Gauhati 1977

Ham, P. van, *Auf Buddhas Pfaden. 2000 km durch den Westhimalaya*, Munich 1994

Ham, P. van, A. Stirn: *Forgotten Gods of Tibet. Early Buddhist Art in the Western Himalayas*, Paris 1997

— *Buddhas Bergwüste. Tibets geheimes Erbe im Himalaya*, Graz 1999

Heine-Geldern, R. F. v., *Kopfjagd und Menschenopfer in Assam und Birma und ihre Ausstrahlung nach Vorderindien. Anthrop. Gesellsch. in Wien*, Vol. 47. 1917

Hodson, T. C.: *The Meitheis*, London 1908

— *Head-hunting among the Hill Tribes of Assam*, Folklore, Vol. 20, 1909

— *The Naga Tribes of Manipur*, London 1911

Hutton, J. H., *The Sema Nagas*, London 1921

— *The Angami Nagas*, London 1921

— *The Meaning and Method of the Erection of Monoliths by the Naga Tribes*, Journal of the Royal Anthropological Institute, Vol. 52. 1922.

— *Diaries of two Tours in the Unadministered Area East of the Naga Hills*, Memoirs of the Asiatic Society of Bengal, Vol. 11.1, 1929

Izzard, R., *The Hunt for the Buru*, London 1951

Jacobs, J., *The Nagas: Hillpeoples of Northeast India*, Stuttgart, London 1990

Khokar, M., *Dancing for Themselves. Folk, Tribal and Ritual Dance of India*, New Delhi 1987

Kowall, E. & N., *Meghalaya*, Hong Kong 1995

Kükelhaus, H., *Urzahl und Gebärde. Grundzüge eines kommenden Maßbewußtseins*, Zug 1984

Lalrimawia: *Mizoram. History and Cultural Identity*, Gauhati 1995

Levine, N., *A Yearbook of Buddhist Wisdom*, New Arlesford 1996

Lianhmingthanga, *A Brief Account on Riangs in Mizoram*, Aizawl 1986

Luczak, H., *Das Reich der Frauen*, In: GEO, Vol. 9, 1995

Madeisky, U., K. Werner, *Die Töchter der sieben Hütten. Matriarchat beim Volk der Khasi in Indien*, Frankfurt 1997 (documentary film)

Mills, J. P., *The Rengma Nagas*, London 1935

— *Head-hunting among the Mishmis of the Lohit Valley*, Assam, Man in India, Vol. 27. 1947

Naga Institute of Culture (Govt. of Nagaland) (ed): *The Arts and Crafts of Nagaland*, Kohima 1968

Nalin, P., *The Nagas*, Paris 1995 (documentary film)

Niyogi, T. K., *Folktales and Myths of Riang and Tripuri communities*, Calcutta 1983

Pakrasi, M., *Folk Tales of Assam*, New Delhi 1972

Peissel, M., *Die Chinesen sind da! Der Freiheitskampf der Khambas*. Vienna, Hamburg 1973

Quinn, D., *Ismael*, Munich 1992

Riba, M., *The Donyi-Poloism*. (Lecture held at the 29th IARF Congress), Seoul, South Korea 1996

Rinpungpa, *Der Bote des Wissens*, In: **Bernbaum, E.**, *Der Weg nach Shambala*, Hamburg 1982

Robinson, W., *A Descriptive Account of Assam to which is added a Short Account of Neighbouring Tribes*, London 1841

Sandys, E. F., *History of Tripura*, Calcutta 1915

Sangkima, *Mizos. Society and Social Change*, Gauhati 1992

Sangma, D.R., *Jadoreng. The Psycho-Physical Culture of the Garos*, Gajingpara 1993

Schicklgruber, C., Pommaret, F. (ed), *Bhutan, Fortress of the Gods*, London 1997

Schuster, C., E. Carpenter, *Patterns that Connect. Social Symbolism in Ancient and Tribal Art*, New York 1996

Sema, H., *Emergence of Nagaland. Socio-economic and Political Transformation and the Future*, New Delhi 1986

Shrivastava, L. R. N., *Among the Wanchos of Arunachal Pradesh*, Shillong 1973

Singh, K. S. (ed) *People of India. a) Vol. 14: Arunachal Pradesh; b) Vol. 31: Manipur; c) Vol. 32: Meghalaya; d) Vol. 33: Mizoram; e) Vol. 34: Nagaland; f) Vol.41: Tripura*, Calcutta 1994-1998.

Thanga, L. B., *The Mizos. A Study in Racial Personality*. Gauhati 1978

Thansanga, H., *Paite in Mizoram*, Aizawl

Trungpa, C., in: **Levine, N.**, *A Yearbook of Buddhist Wisdom*, New Arlesford 1996

Uhlig, H., *Am Anfang war Gott eine Göttin. Eine Weltreligion des Weiblichen*, Bergisch-Gladbach 1995

Varman, S. B., *The Tribes of Tripura*, Agartala 1986

Verghese, B. G., *India's Northeast Resurgent. Ethnicity, Insurgency, Governance, Development*, New Delhi 1996

Whitehead, J. (ed), *Himalayan Enchantment*, London 1990

Northeast India:
Travel Information

General
The northeast of India is one of the wettest regions of the world. The intense flooding of the summer monsoon season makes it practically inaccessible during May through September. The best season to travel is from October through April with temperatures ranging from around –10°C at night in the high hills of Nagaland and Arunachal, to 35°C in the plains of Assam and Tripura. Several northern areas of Arunachal (e.g. Tawang) may not be reachable in winter due to snowfall.

Permits
(Source: The Government of India Tourist Department. Valid as of July 2000)

Of the seven northeastern states discussed in this book (Sikkim only recently became part of the Northeast), only three are open to individual foreign tourists: Assam, Meghalaya and Tripura. Due to possible political disturbances, be prepared for checks at airports or hotels.

In Arunachal Pradesh, Nagaland, Manipur and Mizoram, travel regulations for foreigners are subject to change according to political circumstances. Indian citizens require Innerline Permits, obtainable either from the Deputy Commissioner of the specific district, or the Resident Commissioner. In Arunachal, itineraries for foreigners (groups of four—or more—with a Government-recognized travel agent) are limited to Sejusa, Tipi, Bhalukpong, Itanagar, Ziro, Daporijo, Along, Pasighat and Miao (Namdapha National Park). Opening Tawang to foreign goups is under discussion.
In Manipur, tourism is similarly limited to groups and to the valley of Imphal only. Access is by air only from Gauhati, Silchar or Calcutta.
In Mizoram, only groups may travel on direct route to the capital Aizawl via Vairangte and Thingdawl.
For all these itineraries, groups have to apply for Restricted Area Permits (RAP) at the local Indian Missions abroad for a limited period of 10 days (5 days in Manipur), no later than eight weeks before the start of their journey. At the time of going to press, Nagaland was entirely prohibited to foreigners.

Assam: "The Unique Country"
Size: 78.523 sq. km. Population: approx. 23 million. Number of administrative districts: 24. Capital: Gauhati / Dispur (alt. 55m). Area code: 0361. Zip code: 781 007. Assam is the gateway to all northeast Indian states. Several airlines (Indian Airlines, Jet Airways, Sahara) fly to Gauhati from Delhi , Calcutta and Bagdogra (West Bengal) as well as from places of the Northeast (Agartala, Aizawl, Dibrugarh, Dimapur, Imphal, Lilabari, Shillong, Naharlagun). Several other destinations in Assam (Jorhat, Tezpur) can be reached by air from Calcutta (Indian Airlines). Gauhati is also connected by rail to New Delhi, Calcutta, Bombay, Madras, Trivandrum, Bangalore, Cochin, Silchar, Tinsukia and Dibrugarh.

Some road distances:
Shillong 103 km, Kaziranga National Park 217 km, Manas Wildlife Sanctuary 176 km, Dimapur 280 km, Itanagar 420 km, Imphal 487 km, Agartala 599 km, Aizawl 538 km, Gangtok 624 km, Darjeeling 587 km, Calcutta 1182 km and Kohima 342 km.

Hotels in Gauhati:
The Brahmaputra Ashok, MG Road (Tel.: 541064; Fax: 540870), government run, 50 rooms, most with a view of the Brahmaputra River. Double rooms are about $40; suites are about $57. The Belle Vue Hotel, MG road (Tel./Fax: 540847), is older, and overlooks the river through flowering trees. 39 rooms. Double rooms are

about $35. The Raj Mahal, AT Road (Tel.: 522476; Fax: 521559). Fancier and a bit more expensive. Not located on the riverbank. Kaziranga: Wild Grass Resort (Barua Bharan, first floor, MC Road, Uzanbazar, Gauhati, or Tel.: 546827) is tasteful and clean. Double rooms are about $22. Several nearby government lodges are cheaper, with equal access to the park's shuttle bus and elephant ride reservation services. Park fees are more than $20 a person per day for entry and an elephant ride. There is an additional $5 to $7 charge for cameras, depending on size, more for telephoto lenses.

Meghalaya: "The Abode of the Clouds"
Size: 22.429 sq. km. Population: approx. 1.8 million. Number of administrative districts: 8. Capital: Shillong (alt. 1496 m). Area code: 0364; Zip code: 793 001. There is an airport at Umroi, 31 km outside Shillong, which is connected by helicopter service with Gauhati (Assam) and Tura (West Garo Hills). Flights only operate during non-monsoon times, approx. three times a week, but not on a regular basis. Baggage limit: 10 kg.

Hotels in Shillong:
The Pinewood Ashok, Tel.: 223116, Fax: 224176, has 41 rooms and several cottages. Double: approx. $34. A room in a cottage is slightly less. The hotel was built as a convalescent home for World War I soldiers. Rooms alongside the office are charming and clean, with coal fires. Advance reservation advisable. Other hotels are: The Pegasus Crown, Police Bazaar, Tel.: 22667. Double: approx. $20; Alpine Continental, Thana Road, Tel.: 220991, Fax: 220996; Hotel Polo Towers, Oakland Road, Polo Ground, Tel.: 222340, Fax: 220090.

Tripura: "The Land of the Children of the Watergoddess"
Size: 10.486 sq. km. Population: approx. 2.8 million. Number of administrative districts: 3. Capital: Agartala. Area code: 0381; Zip code: 799 001. The capital is connected by Indian Airlines flights to Calcutta, Gauhati, Delhi. The two nearest railway stations are Kumarghat (160 km) and Dharama Nagar (200 km).

Hotels in Agartala:
Rajdhani. B.K. Road. Agartala. Tel.: 223387. Rooms from $10 to $50. Royal Guest House, Palace Compound. Tel.: 225652. Rooms from $8 to $35. Radha International, 54 Central Road. Rooms from $5 to $25. Tel.: 224530.

Arunachal Pradesh: "The Land of the Rising Sun"
Size: 83.743 sq. km. Population: approx. 860.000. Number of administrative districts: 11. Capital: Itanagar (alt. between 200 m (Naharlagun) and 750 m). Area code: 0360; Zip code: 791 110.
If weather permits, the Government of Arunachal Pradesh provides a helicopter service operated by the Pawan Hans Company. Flights run between Gauhati, Naharlagun, Tezu and Dibrugarh. All entry formalities for Arunachal have to be cleared before boarding at Gauhati Airport. 10 kg luggage limit. The nearest railway station is Harmuty (near Banderdewa check gate), 23 km from Naharlagun. However, the nearest convenient station is North Lakhimpur in Assam, 50 km from Naharlagun.

Hotels in Itanagar:
The Donyi Polo Ashok, Sector C, Itanagar, Tel.: 22626, Fax: 22611. 20 a/c rooms. Hotel Bomdila, Tel.: 22664. Large building, nicely located in lower Itanagar. Hotel Arun Subansiri, Zero Point, Tinali, Tel.: 22766

Manipur: "The Bejewelled Land"
Size: 22.327 sq. km. Population: approx. 1.9 million. Number of administrative districts: 9. Capital: Imphal (alt. 790 m.). Area code: 0385; Zip code: 795 001. Imphal is connected to Delhi, Calcutta and Gauhati by Indian

Airlines and Jet Airways. The nearest railway station is Dimapur, 215 km away.

Hotels in Imphal:
Hotel Excellency, Airport Road, Imphal. Tel: 225401, Fax: 222936. Double: $15. Pretty much the only hotel in town with fine rooms and attentive service. Other hotels are: Imphal, Prince and White Palace.

Mizoram: "The Country of the Highlanders"
Size: 21.081 sq. km. Population: approx. 640.000. Number of administrative districts: 3. Capital: Aizawl (alt. 1374 m.). Area code: 0389; Zip code: 796 001. The airport near Aizawl is nearing completion.

Hotels in Aizawl:
Tourist Lodge. Chaltlang. Aizawl. Tel.: 20206.

Nagaland: "The Land of the Nagas"
Size: 16.579 sq. km. Population: approx. 1.2 million. Number of administrative districts: 7. Capital: Kohima (alt. 1495 m.). Area code: 0386; Zip code: 797 001. Nearest airport and railway station are Dimapur, 74 km from Kohima.

Hotels in Kahima:
Japfu Ashok. Tel: 2721.
Ambassador. Tel.: 444.
Tourist Lodge. Tel: 2417.

Tourist Information Centers in NE-India:
Government of India Tourist Offices:
1 B.K. Kakati Road, Ulubari, Gauhati, Assam. Tel.: 547407.
2 Tirot Singh Syiem Road, Police Bazar, Shillong, Meghalaya. Tel.: 225632.
3 Jail Road, Imphal, Manipur. Tel.: 21131.
3 Sector-C, Naharlagun, Arunachal Pradesh. Tel.: 371.

State Government Tourist Offices:
1 Director of Tourism, Govt. of Assam, Station Road, Ulubari, Gauhati. Tel.: 527102.
2 Kaziranga Wild Life Sanctuary, P.O. Kaziranga 785 109, Assam. Tel: 23.
3 Directorate of Tourism, Govt. of Meghalaya, MTC Building, Top floor, Shillong 793 001, Tel.: 22-6054, 22-6220.
4 Directorate of Information, Cultural Affairs & Tourism, Govt. of Tripura, Swet Mahal Palace Compound, Gandhighat, Agartala Tel.: 22-5930, 22-3839.
5 Public Relations and Tourism, Govt. of Arunachal Pradesh, Sector-C, Naharlagun, Tel.: 371.
6 Tourist Information Center, Directorate of Tourism, Govt. of Manipur. Jail Road, Imphal. Tel.: 224603.
7 Director Tourism Department, Govt. of Mizoram. Aizawl. Tel.: 21226 /7/8.
8 Office of the Public Relations Officer, Nagaland House, 29 Aurangzeb Road, New Delhi 110 011. Tel.: 011-3012296.

Travel Agents
Our journeys have been excellently planned by the Departments of Tourism of the Governments of Assam, Tripura and Mizoram. They arrange tours according to clients' interests. For our other journeys we worked with the following companies, whose services we can highly recommend:

Donyi Hango Adventure Tours and Travels
Yane and Ozing Dai, C-Sector, Naharlagun, Arunachal Pradesh 791 110. Tel.: 0360-244977. Fax: 2446944

Cultural Pursuits
James M. Perry and Somu John, Mawlai, Nongpdeng, Shillong 793008, Tel.: 0364-229016, 250573. Fax: 221816, www.culturalpursuits.com

The Authors

The authors and photographers, Dr. Aglaja Stirn (left)
and Peter van Ham (far right), have been travelling in Asia
for the last two decades. Over the years, they have set
their focus on the less explored regions of India and the
Himalayas, with the aim of documenting unique and
otherwise extinct lifestyles, traditions, customs and the art
of people that represent minorities in their countries. Their
pioneering research has lead to three books and a great
number of articles on the remote and inaccessible Indo-
Tibetan border region of the western Himalayas. Their
photographs are published internationally in renowned print
media and film. Due to the reputation earned from their
work, they were granted special permits by the Indian
authorities, enabling them to do their fieldwork in India's
Northeast over a period of five successive years. In Germany,
Dr. Aglaja Stirn is the assistant medical director of the Frankfurt University Hospital for psychosomatic medicine and psy-
chotherapy. She has been working as a doctor in
the U.S., India and Nepal. Peter van Ham, who studied
music in Los Angeles, works as a teacher in Frankfurt and
has presented multimedia performances and exhibitions all
over Europe, as well as producing music and film scores.

Photographic Credits

All photographs by Aglaja Stirn and Peter van Ham with the
exception of the following:

Bernard, P.: pp. 28 top r., 30, 31, 42, 48 r., 49 r.,
    55 bottom l., 81, 122 bottom l.
Bower, U. G.: p. 40 l.
Brauns, C. D.: p. 128
Dept. of Information and Public Relations, Govt. of
    Arunachal Pradesh: pp. 18, 19, 20, 21, 36 r., 40 r., 41,
    46 l., 47, 68, 69, 87
Dilwali, A.: pp. 56, 109
Ernsting, T. / Bilderberg: pp. 44 bottom, 98 top l.
Gessinger, G.: pp. 38, 57 2nd from top, 111
Gomille, A.: p. 126 top l.
Horter, G.: pp. 16 top l., 25 bottom l., 55 top l., 58 top. r.,
    bottom r., 102, 104. bottom r., 106 bottom l., bottom r.,

115, 123 center r., 127 bottom in center, 130 r., 131
    bottom l., 142 center l, bottom, 149 bottom l., 157
    top. r., back cover
Govt. of India Tourist Offices: pp. 26 top l., 46 r., 73 r., 82 l.,
    91 top, bottom center, bottom l., 127 top l., center l.
Nalin, P.: 2/3, 33, 48 top l., bottom center, bottom, 53
    bottom, 55 r. 2nd from top, 66 bottom l., bottom r., 127
    center r., bottom r., 129 top r., bottom r., 130 l., 136,
    137, 139, 140 top r., 142 top r., bottom r.,
    145 bottom r., 146, 147, 150 center top, right, 151
Nath, A.: pp. 27 top r., 70 2nd from top, 71 all illus. r., 86
    top l., 104 top r., 113, 149 center l., 157 top l., bottom
Patel, V. J.: p. 49 l.
Sanghvi, H. C.: pp. 26 bottom l., 57 top, 72 top l., 99 top r.,
    119, 142 top l., 143
Shah, P.: pp. 92, 93 top r., center r.

Naga – Songs from the Mist

During their comprehensive fieldwork in Northeast India, the
authors were also able to record traditional music of the
indigenous people they encountered. These tribal songs,
dances and rhythms, placed into a Western musical setting
by Peter van Ham and the renowned German composer
Tilmann Höhn, may be heard on the CD "NAGA - Songs
from the Mist". This unique world-music project is available
in your local record store or see the authors' website:
http://www.stirn-vanham.com